MINORITIES and POLITICS

MINORITIES

and

POLITICS

Edited by
Henry J. Tobias
and
Charles E. Woodhouse

UNIVERSITY OF NEW MEXICO PRESS • ALBUQUERQUE

CONTENTS

CHARLES E. WOODHOUSE
Minorities and Politics: An Introduction   1

HENRY J. TOBIAS
The Jews in Tsarist Russia: The Political
Education of a Minority   19

MARCEL RIOUX
Quebec: From a Minority Complex to Majority
Behavior   39

FRANCES L. SWADESH
The Alianza Movement of New Mexico: The
Interplay of Social Change and Public
Commentary   53

SUZANNE L. SIMONS
The Cultural and Social Survival of a Pueblo
Indian Community   85

ROGER W. BANKS
Between the Tracks and the Freeway:
The Negro in Albuquerque   113

CONTRIBUTORS   133

MINORITIES and POLITICS

CHARLES E. WOODHOUSE

MINORITIES AND POLITICS
An Introduction

More than twenty years ago Louis Wirth, in a wide-ranging essay comparing the types of social movements characteristic of minorities in the modern world, classified these movements according to their typical aims. Minorities can be pluralistic, seeking toleration for their own way of life along with full civil and economic rights in the host society. If successful in this they may then seek full assimilation. But if frustrated in this aim, they may seek complete separation from the dominant society either by establishing a new nation of their own or by joining another nation with which they identify more closely. Should they make progress toward these latter objectives, they may become militant, seeking to dominate other groups; and if successful they may cease to be treated as minorities and cease to regard themselves as such.[1]

Wirth offered his typology as "a theoretical construct, rather than as an exact description of actually existing groups." [2] Yet he was particularly interested in the political significance of the "life cycle" of minorities set forth in this typology. Writing at the end of World War II, he was acutely aware of the dangers to international peace which had been created by minority movements in the past. These dangers had developed during the nineteenth century, growing out of eighteenth-century doctrines of democracy which emphasized the right of all peoples to self-government but which also gave rise to nationalistic aspirations on the part of

1

cultural minorities. The fact that political and ethnic boundaries seldom ever coincide had produced internal strains in newly formed nations and these strains had contributed materially to the onset of both world wars. But Wirth looked forward to the possibilities that the advance of science and the trend toward secularism would reduce the virulence of intergroup prejudice, and that the application of enlightened social policy would lead to the solution of the political problems posed by minority groups.[3]

From the vantage point of our own generation we can reassess these problems and from that reassessment develop theoretical insights which go beyond the specification of types of minority movements and stages in the "life cycle" of minorities. We have become concerned today with the processes of nation-building set in motion since World War II with the withdrawal of colonial power from large areas of Asia, Africa and the Near East, and with the political integration of older nations as they meet the new strains of international competition and advanced industrialization. Within our own borders, for example, we see American Negroes being mobilized as a minority whose "militancy" does not stem from acquiring independence or political power but rather from their frustration at the failure to become assimilated into American society. In the new nations beyond our borders we see the upsurge of minority aspirations as a problem in the political integration of those societies. By comparing these broad developments, and looking at the contexts within which minority movements take on political significance, we should be able to carry forward the historical and comparative approach which Wirth undertook.

In a provocative essay, Clifford Geertz has depicted the "integrative revolution" now in process in the new states of Asia, Africa and the Near East. A critical problem in the political integration of these new states is created by the quickening of "primordial ties" among the peoples who have resided in these areas under colonial rule and who now face the opportunity for governing themselves. These primordial ties—of kinship, language, region, religion and custom—now form the basis for separatist, irredentist and factional movements within the new states as groups who share these ties bid for recognition. They are asserting claims to political power and to cultural rights which had not been recognized under colonial rule but which are now established as the price of developing the civic unity that a modern nation requires. The basic structure of political power in these new states is threatened by these drives for separate recognition on the part of minorities.[4]

In comparative perspective, the role of minorities in the nation-building process on the North American continent appears to be the opposite of what is happening in the new nations during the twentieth century. Canada and the United States are nations built upon the absorption of successive waves of immigrants. With the exception of the French colonists in Quebec and Louisiana, and the Spanish and Mexican settlers in the Southwest, the ethnic and religious minorities could not effectively challenge the hegemony of the national state on the ground of separate rights deriving from prior or indigenous claims to territory, status or cultural autonomy. Instead, the immigrant minorities for the most part sought to be accepted within an established political framework different from the one in their homeland. These immigrant minorities were consciously or unconsciously committed to sociocultural assimilation. Insofar as they attempted to retain their sense of ethnic and cultural identity, they had to do so as citizens loyal to the nation.

A condition basic to the adjustment of immigrant minorities has been the displacement of interest in the preservation of ethnic identity—a "status" interest as Max Weber would term it—by interest in economic advancement and political power on an equal basis with all citizens of the nation—in other words by what Weber would call "class" interests. The assimilation of minorities has been facilitated by their absorption into the labor force, into unions which could bid collectively for economic gains; and by the minorities' absorption into political parties where they could bid for a share of power and patronage. At the same time the separation of church and state and the resulting religious freedom permitted the minorities to preserve a sense of group identity which did not conflict with the basic pluralism of the society at large. So long as an ethnic minority could believe its interests in economic advancement and political power were not being blocked by cultural discrimination, the preservation and recognition of cultural identity by the larger society did not become a political or economic issue.

From this comparison of North America with the new nations of Asia, Africa and the Near East it could be inferred that so long as these new nations lack an industrial economy which permits the development of class interests and the means to express them, the aspirations of minorities will continue to be phrased as status interests, which can only be satisfied by the division of political power. Here we arrive at the dilemma which confronts the new nations. Since industrialization requires a sense of political citizenship which permits cultural strangers to come to terms with one another, the blockage of political unity by quickened minority aspirations hampers the development of class interests.

But if this dilemma is characteristic of the new nations, does it mean that the older nations have solved the problem of national integration just because they are industrialized? Is the preservation of ethnic identity, or the struggle for recognition of the rights of minorities by political means no longer likely or possible in industrial societies?

The answer is clearly no. As the pace of economic development proceeds in industrial societies, they develop their own characteristic problems. The economic development and urbanization which industrialization fosters, involve a continuous upgrading of the labor force. Fewer people are employed in agriculture and more people are employed in professions, government, communications and marketing than are employed in the manufacturing sector of the economy. This cycle reduces opportunities for work in unskilled jobs at the same time that it increases the educational requirements for skilled occupations. Thus, deprived minorities can suffer a further relative deprivation of economic opportunity. This deprivation is aggravated by the gains in status and wealth enjoyed by those equipped for the higher incomes available in the "tertiary" (services) sector of the economy. In the United States the recognition of this relative deprivation—in rural areas such as Appalachia, among Spanish-Americans in the Southwest and among Negroes throughout the country—has become so acute that it has provoked a "War on Poverty."

The "War on Poverty" is a phrase coined by the government. It signifies an obligation to guarantee the basic rights of modern citizenship, including equal economic opportunity. The discharge of this obligation involves the framing of legislation, the provocation of disputes over governmental policies and the mobilization of partisans on all sides for one or another solution to the problems of people who are left behind in the course of economic advance. Thus minorities become involved in politics when their class interests become the object of governmental concern. When these interests are phrased in political terms, such as those employed by the Spanish-Americans of New Mexico in "The Alliance of Free City States" or by the American Negroes as "Black Power," the implication is clear that political rather than economic means are regarded as most appropriate for the realization of minority aspirations.

This is the problem which has inspired the collection of essays in this volume: that of surveying the conditions under which minorities interpret their situations in the larger society as ones in which political considerations become relevant or as situations in which political considerations become or remain irrelevant to status interests. How do minorities become involved with politics in a quest for cultural identity, or in an effort to preserve that identity? Or, conversely, how do minorities become involved in a quest for cultural identity as a result of their political involvement?

If minorities assume that they are being economically or politically deprived because of the cultural or racial difference between themselves and the larger society, they can become involved in politics because they believe that the exertion of influence on government is necessary to achieve their objectives. Because effective political action requires unity among people suffering from the same deprivations, minorities can become concerned with a need to define their distinctive claims to status. Unity can be engendered by reminding people of, and infusing with value, the cultural characteristics which they share.

More than the fact of deprivation or oppression, however, is necessary before these contingencies can become motives for action. What is also necessary is the awareness that pressure on government has some promise of success, that it will in fact make a difference, and the awareness that unity can in fact be achieved by reminding people of what they have in common. These two levels of awareness cannot be taken for granted in any historical situation; they develop under specific conditions which can be distinguished from the oppression being suffered.

One set of these conditions may be characterized as the "inflation of opportunity." It is an intervening variable between oppression and collective action. It occurs when a minority acquires new ideas about its position in society that contradict assumptions previously held about the inherent justice or inevitability of its subordination, or when other groups in the society begin openly to question the structure of power and status which has served to maintain their subordination. Either or both of these conditions can serve to alter the minority's perspective on the possibility for change in its position and its fortunes.

Henry Tobias shows us how this inflation of opportunity affected the politics of the Jews in Tsarist Russia. Russia occupied an intermediate position between the situation of the new nations depicted by Geertz and the situations of Canada and the United States. Like the new nations, Russia's minorities were already residing within her borders when the social changes occurred which altered their opportunities for self-assertion. Like the United States and Canada, she was undergoing the processes of modernization and industrialization which would also bring class interests to the fore. Tobias shows how oppression by the Tsarist regime was not enough to bring about revolutionary activity among the Jews, and that it was not until the 1870's that revolutionary interest was aroused. This resulted from their admission to universities, from secular movements within their communities and from the introduction of Marxism to Russia. The increasing industrialization of Russian society and the changes set in motion by the emancipation of the serfs in 1861 allowed the Jews to identify themselves with the Russian working class in a revolutionary movement.

The central significance of Jewish political activism, as Tobias points out, consists in the crisis of identity which required Jews to reconcile their Jewishness with the possibility of new modes of life—either in a Jewish homeland abroad, or in the democratic West, or within a Russian state altered by revolution. The range of options brought into view by the revolutionary ferment in Russia provided the Jews with alternative solutions to their problem as a minority. Paradoxically, the most radical solutions proved to be the most viable while those which appeared most practical at the time eventually bore little fruit.

The conditions opposed to those which constitute an inflation of opportunity are those which constitute a "constriction of opportunity." Here the awareness of oppression on the part of a minority is brought about by the imposition of some limitation upon the freedom or autonomy which the members have previously enjoyed. What is essential is that the minority is unable to remove this limitation and begins to act on the assumption that it cannot be removed. Deprived of their former status, the members seek to redefine their new status in terms of beliefs and practices which distinguish them from their oppressors. This redefinition may consist of the claim to a distinctive cultural identity which the minority then seeks to preserve through its own institutions.

Such a case is that of the French who settled in Quebec in the seventeenth century. Unlike the Jews, who had no territory to which they could lay claim as a minority, the French originally held what later became one province among others in Canada under British domination. In "Quebec: From a Minority Complex to Majority Behavior," Marcel Rioux shows how this territorial base supplied the French-Canadians with a means for retaining a traditional way of life and for culturally isolating themselves from the rest of the Dominion. Instead of seeking to redefine their identity in terms that were compatible with modernization and with the development of a new nation, the French-Canadians in Quebec—in a manner strongly reminiscent of the Boers of South Africa when beleaguered by the British—built a conception of themselves based on strong religious ties and an isolated life as rural peasants. Their politics was thus a politics of self-exclusion from the claims on loyalty made by the nation at large.

Rioux shows further how this self-excluding politics of the French-Canadians has become transformed. In that transformation the behavior of French-Canadians, who began in 1945 to challenge the dominance of the old elites in Quebec, resembles the efforts of those Jews in Russia who sought to redefine their cultural identity—without losing it—in terms compatible with modernization and with participation in a wider national community. Schisms appear between the champions of what Rioux calls the "catching up" ideology, and the clergy and the liberal professions in Quebec, analogous to those which divided religious leaders and conservative traditionalists from the young Jewish intellectuals and revolutionaries in Russia. Likewise a suggestive parallel develops between the role of Henri Bourassa in Quebec and that of Simon Dubnow in Russia, the former seeking a political rapprochement between Quebec and Canada and the latter seeking a philosophical reconciliation of Jewish identity with modern political life.

While it would appear that economic development and political integration leave the partisans of Quebeçois nationalism to pursue their cause through separatist parties with only a minor role in the politics of Quebec, still another picture is presented by the Spanish-Americans of the American Southwest. Here national economic development has widened the gap between a flourishing urban Anglo population and a segment of the Spanish-American population still clinging to the hope of a rural economy based on grants of land which they claim have been unjustly taken from them. From this standpoint, the Alianza movement appears as a response to relative deprivation. But from the standpoint of the Spanish-Americans' political history, the Alianza movement appears to be a response to the inflation of opportunity.

Like the French in Canada, the Spanish-Americans gained land of their own by settling in areas of what is now the American Southwest. But unlike the French, for whom Quebec became a cultural stronghold, the Spanish-Americans were unable politically or culturally to dominate the territory after it was ceded to the United States by Mexico. As Frances Swadesh reviews their history in "The Alianza Movement of New Mexico," she also shows what little regard the rest of the United States had for the significance of the Spanish-American settlers before New Mexico became a state. While there is a parallel here with the chauvinism of the British expressed by Lord Durham toward the French after the Rebellion of 1837–38, still no one found in the Territory of New Mexico, as he did in Quebec, a "struggle, not of principles, but of races." The Spanish-Americans simply did not have enough power to pose the problem for the Anglos that the French in Quebec posed for the British. And the final admission of New Mexico to statehood did not elevate the Spanish-Americans to the political status which the French-Canadians have held in Canada.

Thus, while the politics of the French-Canadians hinged on the relationship of a province to the Dominion, Spanish-American politics was not oriented toward the relation of New Mexico to the United States. Moreover it is questionable whether Spanish-American participation in politics up to the time of the Alianza movement was even strongly motivated by a sense of cultural distinctiveness vis-à-vis Anglo society. Spanish-American political leaders, in a manner similar to those of immigrant minorities elsewhere in the United States, drew support and won patronage in the party system on the basis of their local backing in Spanish-American communities. They have not done so, however, in the same way as in Quebec—as representatives of a self-conscious minority anxious to preserve its culture.

That is why the efforts of Reies Tijerina and his followers signify something more than a bid for the restoration of lost land grants. They represent a departure for the Spanish-Americans from an old style of localistic politics to a new style. This new style results from an inflation of opportunity created by the political atmosphere of the United States in the 1960's. The "War on Poverty" and the flurry of civil rights measures represent an open acknowledgement that in the most prosperous period of our history wrongs exist which ought not to be tolerated. Sit-ins, student protests, antiwar and civil rights demonstrations, activist intervention in the struggle to secure Negro voting rights, all set a model for "confrontation" politics. The leaders of the Alianza have not missed the cues.

The new style of politics in the Alianza movement is a bid for power and recognition in a political arena which transcends the villages in the northern counties of New Mexico and the Spanish-American enclaves in the cities. This requires a sense of unity that goes beyond the local ties of neighborhood and family upon which party politics has been based. Since domination of a territory is lacking as a basis for unity, the appeal for recognition of a distinctive cultural identity could thus serve a function for the Alianza movement. But the assimilation of great numbers of Spanish-Americans to Anglo society has left few institutional resources available for a cultural renaissance. Without schools under their own control and without an indigenous literary elite, the principal media for cultivating a sense of cultural identity among Spanish-Americans are the traditionalistic kinship networks, small local newspapers and Spanish-American radio broadcasting facilities.

In view of this tenuous institutional base, it is not surprising that the Alianza leaders have also sought support for their movement by linking their cause with the Anglo poor and with the Indians and the Negroes in the pan-ethnic appeal to which Swadesh alludes. Faced with a choice between the strategy of a cultural renaissance and the strategy of a class struggle, there is some question, as Swadesh points out, whether the leadership has the means to carry the movement beyond the stage of court trials and legal maneuvers.

All of the studies thus far—the Jews in Russia, the French-Canadians of Quebec and the Spanish-Americans of New Mexico —exhibit a dynamic relationship between politics and changes in a minority's conception of itself. In striking contrast is the case of a Pueblo Indian community in New Mexico, which exhibits a remarkable equilibrium in its self-conception and in its adjustment to the political environment. In one of the rare glimpses we have of an American Indian community in its adaptation to the "Great Society," Suzanne Simons shows how a stable self-conception is sustained and how a distinctive minority culture can preserve itself within the very orbit of the largest city in the state.

Undoubtedly, what makes this balance possible is the unquestioned and unthreatened right to land which is held collectively by the members of the Indian community. Given this security, the community enjoys a range of options in its adjustment to the economic changes taking place in the surrounding non-Indian society. The Indians can live in two worlds—that of the nearby city, where they find employment in modern enterprises, and the world of the pueblo, where they can pursue their traditional family life and religious rites without interference or distraction.

What seems to be as valuable a resource as the land itself is the

intricate structure of social ties which binds families together for
ceremonial occasions, and interlocks the political, religious and
judicial functions performed by community leaders. The strong
and clearly developed sense of membership in the community is
amply illustrated by the lives of those who marry into the pueblo
from other places. Through institutions of mutual aid, this intricate network of social relationships (plus the sense of membership which they reinforce) works to relieve the members of individual economic dependence on the outside world.

From our comparative standpoint it is interesting to note the
contrast between the Pueblo Indians' lack of any sense of identity
with other minorities in American society, and the deliberate pan-
ethnic orientation of the Spanish-American Alianza leadership.
From the perspective which Simons provides, however, it would
seem that the Indians have their own separate channels through
which to deal with the outside society: through the All Indian
Pueblo Council, the Bureau of Indian Affairs, and the Office of
Economic Opportunity. Indians by and large seem to have developed a greater reliance on their own institutions of self-
government and upon federal agencies—in short a more bureau-
cratic relationship to the larger society than any other American
minority.

Long contact with the federal government in handling community affairs has developed a generation of Indian leaders capable
of dealing effectively with other large-scale organizations in
American society. The most recent examples of this are the successful efforts of Indians to secure educational facilities and con-
sultative services for economic development through Indian Centers at major universities, not only in the United States but also
in Canada. This is, however, a modus operandi that can succeed
only as long as Indian leaders are secure in the backing of the
people whom they represent, a backing that would seem to be
assured by the survival of communities with internal solidarity of
the type which Simons describes.

The other American minority which has had as much attention

from the federal government as the Indians is the Negro. Unlike the Indians, however, Negroes have not had a life in autonomous local communities. With this we come to a paradox which is created by the structure of the American political system and the Negroes' position in it. This is the paradox of pluralism. It consists in the fact that on a national level there is a commitment to guarantee the Negro's civil rights and his equal opportunity for education and employment. But the structure of the American political system is such as to render empty all of the gains made by Supreme Court decisions and Congressional legislation if these are not implemented at local levels where the authority must be exercised (witness local school boards resisting desegregation) and where consensus must be mobilized to assure compliance.

Nationally, at the level where such organizations as the NAACP, the National Urban League, SCLC and CORE have had their greatest publicity impact, the Negroes are relatively strong. Locally, however, with the exception of a few large northern cities where they have become important in party politics, the Negroes are weak. What they lack is the social solidarity that political strength requires. "Black Power" and Martin Luther King's nonviolent resistance are both responses to this lack of solidarity. This is equally true of the movement to develop a sense of Negro cultural identity, whether this is based on efforts to introduce Negro and African history courses in universities or on the doctrine of the Black Muslims.

One of the more extreme examples of this lack of local strength appears in Roger Banks' essay, "Between the Tracks and the Freeway: The Negro in Albuquerque." He looks beyond the fact that Negroes constitute less than two per cent of Albuquerque's population, and calls attention to two other conditions which make that weakness even more acute. One is the virtual absence of leadership among middle-class Negroes on behalf of more impoverished Negroes. The other condition is the presence of the larger minority of Spanish-Americans, and with this situation the paradox of pluralism comes most glaringly into view. What

Banks shows is the competitive disadvantage of the Negro when federal assistance through the "War on Poverty" is made available at the local level.

In a comparative perspective the prospects for Negroes may be viewed in terms of what means are available and what the incentives are for Negroes to develop political strength. This question becomes relevant as prospects seem dim for the kind of economic improvement that has aided the assimilation of other minorities. Indeed it appears that the precedent has already been set for realizing the Negroes' class interests by political means.

This puts the Negroes in a peculiar situation. Their past experience in slavery has left them without the resources of tradition and culture which have served the interests of political unity in the case of other minorities. Unlike the Jews, the French-Canadians, the Indians and the Spanish-Americans, the Negroes have not had a distinctive language or religion or the institutions which grow out of a common community life. Also they have had no territorial base with which to identify. Although certain music and language forms have become culturally distinctive to Negroes, these by themselves do not supply concrete precedents for collective aspiration and political action. This creates a vacuum into which all manner of self-definitions may be introduced in a search for identity and a search for strategies. At the same time Negroes face resistance from white society in the claims they do advance and the aspirations they do articulate. Thus it is all the more likely that the solutions advanced will be novel and drastic.

Henry Tobias has elsewhere drawn attention to the parallel here between the situation of the Negro in America and that of the industrial proletariat in Russia during the pre-revolutionary period. Compared to the Russian peasants, with whom the Tsarist government had dealt for centuries and who had precedents set in their own village life for dealing with the government, the growing urban industrial proletariat represented a new element in the Tsarist state which the government had not dealt with previously as an entity, and toward which the government reacted with resistance when the workers began to bid for recognition. Characteristically the Tsarist government responded to the workers by acting as if anything the government had not previously allowed them was ipso facto illegal. Apart from a modicum of factory legislation, the only solution the regime attempted was the effort of Zubatov, the Moscow Chief of Police, to provide police leadership for the socialist movement. One factor in the success of the Russian Revolution undoubtedly was the Tsarist government's inability to handle the claims of the urban proletariat.

The reader may imagine what chance there would be in the United States to enlist police leadership, or what chance there would be for Negroes to accept that leadership in the cause of civil rights. It would appear, however, that the "War on Poverty" represents today the same search for an expedient on the part of the government that Zubatovism represented on the part of the Tsarist regime.

On balance, however, it appears that action on the Negro front is likely to occur at the local level from now on. Whether this threatens to be explosive, as in places like Oakland where police and Black Panthers confront each other in all but a state of open warfare, or whether it takes the form of self help projects such as those in the Bedford-Stuyvesant area of Brooklyn, new precedents for collective effort are going to be set. We face a new situation in the process whereby a modern industrial nation confronts the problems of civic integration which minority groups pose.

We can characterize the approach which has guided this comparison of minorities by relating it again to Wirth's typology. In distinguishing types of minority movements and stages in their "life cycles," Wirth implicitly casts minorities in the role of protagonists on the historical scene. He endows them with initiative in choosing a course that leads either to full assimilation in the host society or secession from it and the establishment of independent political power. The conditions of reaching either of these goals are phrased in terms of the host society's response to the minority's own movement. But if we take an opposite view, and consider the conditions created by a host society which determine whether minorities take initiative or not, we see that four distinct variables operate to determine the course which any minority might take. Class interests and status interests, and the inflation or constriction of opportunity appear to function in ways which suggest further problems for theory and research.

Two contrasting examples will illustrate the problematic relationships between these variables. The American Indians and the Negroes both represent cases par excellence of minorities whose initiative on their own behalf has been greatly conditioned by the larger society. Yet they represent quite opposite cases of political involvement.

Sequestered in semiautonomous communities on reservations, Indians have not had to participate as a group in the political life of the nation. To the extent that their lands and other economic resources have continued to be useful and have remained in their own hands, Indians have been insulated from the stratification system of the larger society. They have not been involved competitively in the pursuit of class interests. And the pursuit of their status interests—in the preservation of their own way of life as a socially honorific one—has not been displaced by class interests as in the case of the immigrant minorities.

Negroes, by contrast, have been thrust into politics virtually against their own will. Emancipation from slavery put them into the open labor market. Discrimination and lack of equal opportunity have put them at a competitive disadvantage so severe that the pursuit of their class interests has become a political problem. Their pursuit of status interests—in a search for social identity and an honorific standing in the larger society—involves the need for political solidarity in the national arena.

Thus we see that for the Indians, class interests and status interests are in a relationship of equilibrium with each other while for the Negroes, the relation between these two sets of interests is unstable and dynamic, undergoing change. The balance between class and status interests is thus a perennial contingency affecting minority politics.

Changes in the balance of class and status interests may result from the inflation or constriction of opportunity. The Indians are responding to the latter. They have acted as if the limitations on their mobility in the larger society, as set by the maintenance of reservations and the economic stake in tribal resources, are not likely to be removed; and Indians take pride in the cultural exclusiveness which these limitations make possible. But if their economic base should disappear or if Indians in larger numbers enter new channels of mobility made available by the larger society, they could become vulnerable to the blockage of their class interests in these new channels. If an inflation of opportunity should then occur, the Indians would be theoretically "eligible" for political mobilization.

Negroes, by contrast, are now responding to an inflation of opportunity. They are demanding a local payoff in the rights which have been promised them by federal officials. Riots in the cities have created in white society an apprehension which justifies taking the claims of Negroes more seriously than before. If the Negroes, however, should begin at some point to construe their situation as hopeless, responding as if to a constriction of opportunity, the effect would now be different from the apathy which was earlier induced by segregation and the Jim Crow laws. Without the determination to pursue class interests in a unified way, the incentive for political action would of course be lost; Negroes cannot secede and they have no political territory to defend. But now the precedent has been set for them to develop status interests in the quest for social identity and an honorific self-conception which would set them apart culturally from the whites.

The choice which a minority makes between construing its situation as an inflation or a constriction of opportunity depends on historical developments which are not entirely under its own control. These developments may result from initiative on the part of a government seeking to ensure political support from diverse groups in a nation, or they may result from the effort of dissident groups either to secure reforms or to maintain the status quo in the distribution of wealth or status. Both phenomena are likely to appear in nations committed to democratic rule and the former is likely to appear in totalitarian ones.

At any rate, the drive for national integration sets conditions which cannot be discounted in any attempt to analyze the political role of minority groups. Whether prompted by the creation of new nations embracing culturally diverse peoples within a nonindustrial economy, or by the strains of advanced industrialization in older nations, such historical developments set an appropriate point of departure for comparative study.

NOTES

1. Louis Wirth, "The Problem of Minority Groups," in Ralph Linton (ed.), *The Science of Man in the World Crisis* (New York: Columbia University Press, 1945), pp. 354–364.

2. *Ibid.*, p. 364.

3. *Ibid.*, pp. 364–372.

4. Clifford Geertz, "The Integrative Revolution: Primordial Sentiments and Civil Politics in the New States," in Clifford Geertz (ed.), *Old Societies and New States* (The Free Press of Glencoe, 1963), pp. 105–157.

HENRY J. TOBIAS

THE JEWS IN TSARIST RUSSIA
The Political Education
of a Minority

As a minority issue, the Jewish question occupied first place in
the attentions of the western world from the last decades of the
nineteenth through the first half of the twentieth centuries. From
the pogroms following the assassination of Alexander II of Russia
in 1881 to the Dreyfus trial and its aftermath in France in the
latter Nineties and the first years of the twentieth century; from
the Kishinev pogrom of 1903 to the arrest and ritual murder trial
of Mendel Beilis in the last years before the Great War; from the
new pogroms at the end of World War I through the horrors of
racial anti-Semitism that reached its peak in the "final solution"
of the Nazis in World War II, the condition of the Jew became
symbolic of the treatment of minorities.

For about seventy years Jews had to cope with regimes which
extended the length of the political spectrum from the liberal
democratic to the most autocratic of monarchies and to the tightest
of dictatorships. Within these societies popular and official images
of the Jews ranged as widely as the political natures of the countries themselves—from citizens with equal rights to a useless tribe
which exploited the indigenous population or a racial monstros-
ity which sought to corrupt the purity of existing nations in order

to gain world power for themselves and was fit, therefore, only for extermination. Jews responded to these circumstances in a variety of ways dictated both by the impingement of the external environment upon them and the nature of their own community.

In the last decades of the nineteenth century, the Jews awakened to political action in terms of self-awareness and as members of a wider community. Concepts of religion, civic status, class, and nationhood became features of their thinking as they aspired to alter their collective circumstances. To accomplish their ends they formed many types of organizations—social and economic societies, parties and pressure groups of a less formal nature—and they became part of larger political combinations where they acted either as individuals or as components within those combinations.

The juxtaposition of political oppression, self-consciousness and opportunity makes the Jews a valuable subject as a case study in a world where minority problems are a subject of keen interest and solutions are crucial for harmony. The wide range of responses and aspirations they expressed offers a panorama of what minorities do politically as they face a modern world where populations are drawn into cities, where industrial establishments organize and homogenize human activities, and where education and loyalties syncretize. The activities of the Jews indicate how a distinct group may define and alter itself in light of such new circumstances.

THE JEWS IN TSARIST RUSSIA

The experiences of the Jews in Russia before the revolutions of 1917 form a special chapter in their history and a provocative one in the study of minorities under conditions of adversity and modernization. Until the end of World War I, they formed the largest Jewish community in the world. The cataclysmic events of twentieth-century political life have shattered that community through war, territorial partition, and deliberate policies of destruction arising from a number of sources. How they rediscovered themselves in a larger society seeking, in turn, to rediscover itself provides us with an early example of the multifaceted possibilities for political definition which may occur for a minority.

When the modern era of suffering for the Jews began in the Tsarist Empire, the vast majority of the Jewish community was distinct from the surrounding population. At the turn of the century it numbered between five and six million, comprising three to four per cent of the total population of the Empire. That relatively insignificant figure, however, can be misleading, for the Jews were not evenly distributed through the vast territories of the Empire. They were concentrated into a large residential ghetto called the Pale of Settlement which comprised the western portions of the country, including Belorussia, Lithuania, the western Ukraine, and the Polish territory in which they dwelt before those lands fell into Tsarist hands at the end of the eighteenth century. They lived in these regions by virtue of laws which forbade all but special categories of their population to leave. Within the Pale, too, the distribution of the population was anything but even. In the 1880's the Jews were beginning to concentrate heavily in towns and cities, partly as a result of general economic factors developing in the society and partly because of new legislation which restricted Jews from residing in villages and some frontier areas. In many of the cities of northwestern Russia, they formed an absolute or near majority of the urban population in the Pale.

Legal restrictions upon the Jews, moreover, were not limited to matters of residence; the phrase "except the Jews" concluded many a paragraph of Tsarist regulations. The state, particularly from the early 1880's on, drastically limited educational opportunities for Jewish children in Russian schools and restricted the Jews from practicing certain professions. They were also required to pay special taxes.

The Jews differed sharply from their neighbors. They fostered their own religious life and institutions. They maintained a separate cultural identity, particularly in Belorussia, Lithuania, and

Poland, by speaking Yiddish at home and among themselves, although they generally had some knowledge of the major language of the area in which they lived.

In their socioeconomic characteristics the Jews also differed profoundly from the vast majority of the population of the Empire. Whereas about eighty per cent of the total population of the Empire consisted of peasants, only five per cent of the Jews derived their living from the land; whereas fifteen per cent of the general population engaged in trade and manufacture, almost seventy-five per cent of the Jews were so employed. Thus, the economic structure of the Jewish population was almost the exact reverse of the general population.

Even in towns where Christian and Jew lived together, there was considerable occupational isolation. They did not usually work in the same trades. In some factories, Jews were not admitted because of their customs—the celebration of the Sabbath on Saturday did not suit employers who hired Christian workers with a Sunday holiday. In others, Christian employers frequently would not hire Jewish workers, and Christian workers in some instances would not permit the employment of Jewish workers.

The economic lot of the Jew, as for much of the population of the Empire, was difficult. There were a few Jews of great wealth who lived in, and even outside of, the Pale of Settlement and by the nature of their economic pursuits formed a middle-class element. The bulk of the population, however, found their existence so hazardous that when the threat of physical violence was added to their already precarious economic situation from the 1880's on, they began to emigrate in large numbers. That process continued until it was interrupted by the exigencies of World War I. Although well over a million emigrated, the exodus did not reduce the absolute number of Jews in Russia and provided little economic relief in the heavily overpopulated centers of the Pale. Pauperism and poverty were relieved only slightly by a strong intracommunal network of mutual aid organizations—unions, charitable institutions—by aid from the lucky ones who had escaped to "golden" America, and from western European agencies.

POLITICAL ACTION IN TSARIST RUSSIA

To speak of political action in the Russian Empire is to move beyond the framework of politics generally known in the United States and the western democracies. Until 1905 political parties were illegal and the state regarded as criminal behavior any independent political activity designed to give people a voice in government. The politics of the Tsarist régime were restricted to administrative and court circles and were influenced only very slightly by locally elected councils, called Zemstvos, which were chosen on a narrow franchise and concerned themselves with local issues. Thus, virtually all desire for political change based on the existence of a body politic had to take an extreme form, and the secret and hazardous nature of revolutionary activity in Russia prevented the large-scale organization of political work. Radical political behavior, which consisted largely of creating revolutionary groups, the formation of terrorist groups, or attempts to inculcate radical ideas by some peaceful, if illegal, means, predated conservative or moderate political action.

THE BACKGROUND OF JEWISH POLITICS IN TSARIST RUSSIA

What conditions induced Jews to turn to politics? Traditionally, they were considered the most docile of minorities. The rabbis, conservative and fearful, generally stood for firmly upholding the law of the land. Yet, by 1905, the Jews had created an astonishing number of political movements, some quite imaginative in conception and determined in their action. In addition, a large number of individuals participated as activists in non-Jewish groups.

The answer is complex. Some roots can be traced to the changing nature of the Jewish community itself, changes in Russian society, and, in part, to developments common to all Europe. The break-up, in 1884, of the Kahal, the juridical head of the Jewish community which exercised some autonomous power, was brought about by the deliberate action of the government. Nicholas I regarded the Kahal as a state within a state and an obstacle to the assimilation he considered desirable for Jews. The liberal reforms of Tsar Alexander II in the 1860's opened the universities to Jews, made governmental and professional careers possible, and produced a gentle pressure for the dissolution of the old traditions.

Within the Jewish community itself, new forces arose to challenge the traditional modes of life. The general phenomenon of secularization, which came to Russian Jews from the writings of Western European Jews, began to affect the upper levels of the community. The Haskalah or Enlightenment movement, as it was called, told the Jew to look to the new secular learning ruling Europe, and to be like his fellows about him, at least outside the home. The new knowledge brought discontent with traditional life to many young people and the challenge to old beliefs and practices grew apace throughout the second half of the nineteenth century.

The end of serfdom in 1861 produced a series of changes which were gradually felt throughout the entire society. In the last two decades of the nineteenth century, urbanization and industrial growth led to the rise of new values and new social classes. The government often misunderstood and generally responded too slowly, even to those changes it initiated, thus appearing reactionary and unbending.

THE SPECTRUM OF POLITICAL RESPONSE AMONG THE JEWS

The Jews derived some notions of how to act politically from observing the politics of non-Jewish society in Russia and in Europe. They turned to current ideologies, such as Marxism or variations of national expression. They used these general criteria to examine their own traditions and attempted to rejuvenate them in forms acceptable to the requirements of modern life. The particular lines of action chosen depended on education, class, cultural background, and commitment to the Jewish community itself.

The most important factor in the political education of the Jews was how they concerned themselves with their Jewishness, since the content for the politics of a Jewish minority could exist only on an axis of Jewish identity. Some limits existed to that axis. There were Jews on the extreme boundary who sought the closest kind of assimilation to Russian culture. There were some who went as far as conversion to Christianity. No matter what their politics the converts could not be taken as part of a political spectrum involving Jewishness except in a psychological sense or if one insists upon a racial definition of Jew—an attitude which the Tsarist regime did not recognize.

At the other end of the axis there were those, particularly from the 1880's on, who hoped to escape the exigencies of life in Russia as soon as they could, to find a homeland for the Jews elsewhere. These Zionists had a somewhat closer relation to the political life of the Jews in Russia for the simple reason that they desired a Jewish future and developed strong images of themselves as Jews. For the present, they had to involve themselves with the facts of political life in Tsarist Russia. In another sense, however, those holding Jewish homeland views placed themselves outside the politics of the Empire, as well as outside the Jewish community of Russia, and, therefore, outside the attempt to find a workable politics for their people in Russia. The work of the early Zionists cannot be ignored completely for the political growth of the Jews in Russia. Such thinkers as Ahad Haam, who combined ideas of homeland and spiritual growth in Russia, and Leo Pinsker, who looked to territory as the way toward self-emancipation, sparked discussion. But the hardcore problem of the Jews' political life in Russia remained: how to retain their identity as Jews and, at the same time, to become part of the general society.

The lines by which Jews entered politics in Russia reflect the diversity of response possible in a society with limited opportuni-

ties for political life as compared with the level of participation
known in the democratic West. The early reactions of Jews to
political life in Russia reflected the outer edges of the spectrum.
The first Jews to enter active political life were the university
students who, benefiting from the liberal reforms of Alexander
II, moved out of their traditional environments. Culturally assimilated, the young Jews assumed the political mores and aspirations of the Russians. They had no specific political aims regarding the Jews. Their goals were universal in that they sought
political and other varieties of justice for all inhabitants of the
Empire. In their universalist hopes some saw an opportunity for
Jews to break with their traditions and move into the modern
secular world of which they had become a part. Lev Deutsch, one
of these early revolutionaries who remained active in Russian
circles, explained his feelings in this manner:

> We wanted the Jews to assimilate as quickly as possible;
> everything that smelled of Jewishness called forth among
> many of us a feeling of contempt if not more. . . . We all
> believed that as soon as Jews would begin to speak Russian,
> they would, just as we did, become 'people in general,' 'cos-
> mopolites.' [1]

Although Deutsch's view contained elements of self-awareness
that belied his claim to complete assimilation, he was characteristic of a political type who reappeared frequently on the Russian
scene. Through the end of the Tsarist regime one would find tal-
ented individuals who would not deny their formal identity as
Jews although there was no positive content to their Jewishness.
Such individuals as Julius Martov, Leon Trotsky, and Rosa Lux-
emburg leaned heavily to universalist forms of political expression. The numbers involved in these activities, however, were too
few and too far removed in culture and interest from the Jewish
masses to influence Jewish affairs.

Although there were some signs of a political awakening
among Jewish students in the 1870's, particularly in the Vilno

Teachers' Institute, dedicated to the training of Jewish teachers, it was during the period of pogroms following the assassination of Alexander II in 1881 that political ideas specifically concerned with the continuation of Jewish life appeared. The aforementioned Zionist thinkers of the Eighties and Nineties represent some of these early attempts. The idea of independent nationhood entered the political consciousness of the Russian Jews. But these ideas were largely negative toward the Russian environment, for the answers they offered lay outside of Russia. To them, the Jew would never be wholly accepted by the Gentile world. Until labor and socialist variants of Zionist thought arose in the early years of the twentieth century, most Zionists paid little or no attention to the internal politics of Russia. They sought to get along as best they could, placing their hopes on a better future elsewhere.

These first steps of the Jews' entrance into politics expressed a marked class and educational character. Assimilationist and Zionist thought depended on intellectual rationalization and high-level education beyond that available to the Jewish masses. The sources of inspiration for these ideas were Russian or Western European thought and the average Jew had little access to such learning. The language of the assimilationists was not usually Yiddish, but Russian. The early Zionist thinkers, too, had no love for Yiddish and communicated in Hebrew, Russian, or Western European languages, which had no connection with the Jewish masses.

It was in the Eighties and Nineties, too, that the slowly changing economic character of the Empire opened the way for the growth and acceptance of new movements and doctrines which could alter Russia in accord with socioeconomic developments in the modern world. Marxism, which gathered its first organized Russian converts in the early Eighties, concentrated its attentions on the problems of industrialization in the cities, where most Jews lived. It recognized all workers as equal human beings regardless of ethnic background and it contained messianic optim-

ism which permitted Jewish intellectuals and workers who accepted the doctrine to engage in a cause that promised gains for
all.

During the early and mid-Nineties, Jewish Marxists who lived
in the Pale of Settlement became aware of the readiness of increasing numbers of Jewish workers to accept revolutionary doctrines and activities, and undertook to draw them into a Marxian
awareness of themselves as workers. Since they were able to approach the lower-class Jew only through his own Yiddish culture,
and since the aims of these young Marxist activists sought a solution for the problems of the proletarian Jews in Russia, their
joint efforts produced a movement clearly within the framework
of minority political activity in Russia. The conscious response of
the Jewish workers to their plight and their willingness to accept
a Marxian viewpoint, moreover, produced a chain of logic leading to increased self-awareness. If Jewish workers could gain
equal and honorable status as workers, then they should also have
a similar status as citizens in a new political order. And if they
could gain equal status as citizens then why should they not have
that status as Jews? The latter question, however, would not satisfy Jewish Marxists with strong universalist tendencies.

The major political instrument for carrying the message of
Marxist philosophy into action among the Jewish workers in the
Pale of Settlement was the General Jewish Workers Union in Lithuania, Poland, and Russia (Bund). Formed in a number of
towns in 1897 by those Marxist Jews who had already been labor-
ing to organize Jewish workers, the Bundists rested their hopes on
a revolution which would include the proletariat of all Russia
and expected that their Jewish workers would become filled with
a sense of dignity, not only as men, but as Jews. Marxism, with its
nonnational bias, posed difficulties for the Bundists, for the universalist proletarian point of view prevented easy acceptance of
formal national goals which moved beyond equal civil rights. But
the Bundists nevertheless adopted a national program in 1905
which called for equal national rights. They insisted that the Jew

had the right to be proud of his culture and should be able to develop it on terms equal with all other nationalities of the Russian Empire. Unlike the Zionists, the Bundists based their national program on the existing Yiddish culture, which the Zionists regarded as worthless.

Despite great obstacles, the Bund proved enormously successful in its efforts to arouse a generation of Jewish workers to political consciousness. It became educator, organizer, and in some instances, actual physical defender of the Jewish community, although in the latter category it received support from other organizations including some Zionists and non-Jews. The history of the Bund up to the Revolution of 1905 is the history of Jewish politics in Russia insofar as it sought to change the existing environment and make it liveable for the Jews. The decline of revolutionary activity which followed the partially successful revolt of 1905 brought the Bund to hard times, although it regained strength later and became a force to be reckoned with in independent Poland.

The Bund, by its transmission of the new ideology and its struggle for stronger consciousness of Jews as persons in the general community, differed from earlier political expressions. In accord with its Marxist beliefs it did not seek to represent the Jews as a unit, but only Jewish workers and those who identified with them. Thus the Bundists split the Jewish community into classes and sought to lead Jewish workers into alliance with other Marxist groups. Its commitment to the working masses, moreover, insured dedication to Yiddish, the mass idiom. This led it into direct conflict with both traditional and newly politicized portions of Jewish society which preferred Hebrew or Russian.

The two major tendencies of Jewish politics in early twentieth-century Russia thus rested on complete territorial nationhood or on equal rights for minorities in Russia in a context of economic and social justice for the downtrodden. While the Zionist ideal presented a dimension acceptable to middle-class and nationalist elements, it said little about present action and it contained

shortcomings in terms of universal social justice, as represented
by the Marxist ideal. The Bund's view, on the other hand, while
it represented an approach to dealing with present injustice and
a general line for future development, did not yet satisfy, specifically enough, descriptions of the future of the Jewish community
and refused to concern itself with many traditional paths of Jewish culture.

The deficiencies present in each of these solutions for the Jewish community led each to partake of the other. Socialist ideas
eventually drew the attention of Zionists while some Jewish
Marxists became concerned with territorial solutions. They
sought to crossbreed Marxism and Zionism to form a new movement which would combine the best of both worlds—a homeland
for the Jews and a socialist order in that homeland. That movement received the general name of Labor Zionism.

Labor Zionism acquired a host of variants in the early twentieth century. Among them were groups which could accept only
the territory of Palestine, while others were willing to settle for
territory elsewhere. Uganda and later Argentina attracted their
attention as likely areas for settlement. But territory remained
crucial for them. Positing the Jews as a territorial nation, some
Marxist-Zionists insisted that they—the outsiders in the Diaspora
—could not even develop into true proletarians without a homeland of their own, for they would always be on the fringes of
economic and social life. The structure for true socialism would
have to emerge from a healthy national body—one that must
have its own land.

The wedding of territorial views to a revolutionary spirit
placed many of the new groups in a position where they could not
remain aloof from the growing unrest in Russia. The Kishinev
pogrom of 1903 served notice that no matter how much Jews
might wish to avoid entanglement in politics, they could not
evade their environment. Even fairly conservative Labor Zionists
tried to improve their economic condition. They took advantage
of government efforts to persuade workers to abandon political

aims by offering help in their economic struggles, a phenomenon which received the general appellation of Zubatovism or Police Socialism. But no semilegal strike could satisfy a revolutionary socialist or assuage the violence of a pogrom inspired or permitted by the police. At any rate, elements of Labor Zionism were drawn into the direct struggle with the state even though their ultimate aims lay outside of Russia. They felt bound to resist the tyranny of the Tsarist regime simply because they were socialists. Their revolutionary urges, as well as their dignity as men, would not permit passivity.

Other conceptions arose based on nation, territory, and the working class, but without a Marxist foundation. Seimism, one of the most important of these, denied the Marxist view that nations were in a state of decline. Taking national will as a powerful incentive for existence, the Seimists postulated the reality of the Jewish nation in the Diaspora. They insisted, furthermore, that a fully developed nation would have to emerge from the existing conditions and materials. To some extent, like the Bundists, they saw positive national developments occurring in Jewish life which could lead to an even fuller evolution of nationhood in Russia. They even anticipated the growth of political institutions within Russia where the state might recognize autonomy for the Jews in a Diet or Seim (hence Seimism), a form of parliament with sufficient power to regulate matters related to Jewish life. They retained homeland aspirations, however, in the sense that the ultimate goal was to acquire territory for themselves, the final stage toward the achievement of nationhood.

Those who disregarded the "territorial imperative," however, had a more difficult task of defining the future than the Zionists. They had to find an identity not only as citizens, but as a distinct ethnic minority.

The Bundists, with their proletarian-democratic point of view, placed the issue squarely on the base of existing mass culture and secularization. Emphasizing the continuation and development of that mass culture, they sought guarantees for the future of the

Jews through the general acceptance of principles of national equality and for institutions in the future Russia which would enable the culture to maintain itself. They wanted their own educational institutions, the right to use Yiddish in state institutions, and the right to develop their culture. They described their aim as national cultural autonomy.

While the Bund remained secular (vis-à-vis the old religion) and proletarian, Simon Dubnow, perhaps the greatest of the modern historians of the Jews, analyzed the minority existence of the Jew in terms of a much wider autonomism. Not Marxist, and unwilling to deny any of the sources which had maintained and enriched the continuity of Jewish life over the centuries, Dubnow saw in the historical experience of the Jews a spiritual quality which made them unique among nations. Having lost their territory and their unifying language, having become dispersed, they had nevertheless maintained a national will which appeared to be indestructible. Using the experience of Jewish history, he was prepared to accept all forms of Jewish expression as part of the national heritage despite differences over language, religion, or homeland. The very multitude of forms of expression served as bases for the possible survival of the nation. No specific form was "best." All might serve to enhance the continuing existence of the nation at any given moment. This spiritual Jewish nation, to him, was the highest form of nationality possible—existing apart from any of the specific aspects attributed to the modern definitions of nationhood.

How did Dubnow's autonomism fit into the Russian scene? In effect, he asked that the Jews be allowed to exercise rights as citizens of the country in which they lived and at the same time to maintain their existence as Jews—a position similar in some respects to the Haskalah or Enlightenment of which Dubnow had been a follower.

Not all political activity among the Jews emerged from the radical intelligentsia or working masses. By 1904 the general political awakening in Russia attracted many persons simply interested in gaining equal civic status as an end in itself. Many Jews, usually those materially better off than their fellows and often assimilated to Russian culture, found possibilities for a better future in a democratized Russia without a socialist basis. These political liberals found it easy to join hands with their Russian counterparts. In 1905, under the impetus of the revolutionary days, these liberal Jews combined into a League for the Attainment of Full Rights for the Jewish People of Russia. They placed their hopes on concessions to be made by the Tsarist regime to the revolutionary temper of the times, particularly the Duma created by the October Manifesto—a victory of the Revolution of 1905. Not actually a political party, the Attainers appeared as a pressure group, hoping to pursue their goals through existing political parties and intent on drawing Jewish political groups together. In its aims the League lay closest to the liberal Constitutional Democratic Party (Kadets), a political choice, incidentally, not far from Dubnow's own.

The attitudes of the various revolutionary and liberal parties among the Jews differed greatly during the Revolution of 1905. The Bund, for example, refused to take part in the elections following the October Manifesto, since it felt that the new Duma would clearly be bourgeois in its makeup. Strongly militant, the Bundists hoped for greater revolutionary gains. The Attainers, on the other hand, sought the election of delegates who would support their goal of equal rights for Jews or to elect Jewish candidates if the situation warranted. Areas of mixed population, lacking clear national majorities, allowed the Attainers to pursue a politics of negotiation; the creation of blocs afforded some hope for the election of candidates to the Duma who might help the Jews. Indeed, twelve Jewish deputies actually were elected to that short-lived body.

The elections for the First Duma were a high point in the political experience of the Russian-Jewish community. If the Bund was wrong in hoping for too much from the Revolution, the expectations of the Jewish liberals also proved too optimistic, for the Tsarist regime soon began to restrict what had been forcibly extracted from it during the crisis of 1905. A decline of legal political activity among the Jews followed and a return to large-scale activism occurred only with the overthrow of the Tsarist regime in 1917.

IMMEDIATE EFFECTS AND SUBSEQUENT
MEANING OF THE JEWISH POLITICAL SPECTRUM

Even the brief and fragmentary sketch given here of the activities developed during the last two generations of the Empire indicates how imaginative and committed the Jews of Russia were in working toward their political future. How did these activities affect Jewish attitudes?

There can be little doubt that politicization caused conservative and traditional elements within the community considerable pain and resentment, and they remained a powerful, if gradually weakening factor in Jewish life. There was no way, in light of the conditions which led to the quickening of political life, for them to stop the tide. From their point of view, therefore, the new movements seemed tragic. In part, they blamed violence against the Jews upon the new activities engaged in by the younger radical generation. To the traditionalists, furthermore, the new views were divisive, destructive of the true ways of the fathers and, therefore, the ruin of those who adopted them.

Once the old unity was shattered, the separate interests in the community took their own direction in accord with the changing environment. The Marxist Bund, for example, with its class orientation, undertook to lead only a portion of the Jewish community, the workers, and even defined Jewish culture in terms of those workers, while seeking to integrate them with society in general along economic lines suitable for that one class. The Bund was attacked, on one hand, on the grounds that it brought disunion into the ranks of the Jews and that its secularity was a half-step toward assimilation. On the other hand, the assimilationists attacked it for its insistence on Yiddish culture. The competing viewpoints gave the "Jewish street" the appearance of a political Tower of Babel.

There can be little doubt that in comparison with the relative stability and homogeneity of earlier generations, the last two generations before the fall of the Tsarist state took on a disruptive aspect. But it must also be noted that the developments which took place grew out of the inability of the earlier leaders to cope with the difficulties of the community. Economic problems alone forced relocation, reeducation and reevaluation, straining the old mode of life to the breaking point. The Jews, culturally independent as they were from the surrounding population, were intimately tied to it economically and thus were unable to ignore the changes occurring throughout society at large.

The effects of political activity were astonishing. A large segment of Jewish youth awoke to the demands of modern life and sought to participate in it. Although their efforts produced only small improvements, the activists took their participation seriously, convinced of the efficacy of action in their own behalf. It is also important to note that as these movements grew, they involved an ever greater portion of the total community, either as actual members of organizations or as peripheral supporters. Even for those who did not join, the arguments around them often proved meaningful. In this sense, a considerable portion of the community was drawn into matters of group concern and the search for solutions.

How effective were the political activities of the Jews for the society in which they dwelt? Clearly, even when they banded together they could carry only relatively small influence in the larger picture. The course open to those who identified their future with Russia, therefore, became one of influencing non-Jewish political forces in Russia to see matters as they did, or adopting views which could fit into the patterns being devised by those larger political forces in a manner acceptable to the Jews. Thus, a politics of principle, which maintained at least the minimum standards of what the Jewish groups considered acceptable, found expression in cooperation, negotiation, and, insofar as possible, pressure.

Given the conditions in Russia under the last Tsars, there was no sign that any quick improvement of the lot of the Jews would take place. Indeed, some of the worst instances of anti-Jewish action occurred during the last years of the regime, including the infamous pogroms and the aforementioned ritual murder trials. The fact that Jews engaged in revolutionary activity simply provided the already anti-Semitic government with an opportunity to make life even more difficult for them. For conservative and reactionary Russians, the actions of the Jews merely proved their harmfulness and allowed them to blame many of society's problems upon these alien "Christ-killers." The only modus vivendi for those Jews who sought to avoid politics was to deal with an unfriendly autocracy. Such negotiations took place on the local level where those able to do so protected themselves through bribery, petition, or some special influence.

What did the political efforts of the Jews mean if the results were small and brought reprisal upon them? The benefits lie in the historical epoch following the Great War. The Tsarist regime fell through war and revolution in 1917, destroying the environment in which the political spectrum conceived by the Russian Jews had grown up. It would be incorrect to conclude, however, that these circumstances rendered their work fruitless. On the contrary, most of the political conceptions of necessity rested on a foundation of drastic change and required a new political or territorial environment.

Torn from their original moorings, the movements had to seek fulfillment in new surroundings. The hopes of the Zionists to acquire a homeland became a fact after the First World War. After another war and a holocaust for the East European Jews, that homeland became an independent state. Those who migrated to the democratic west in search of a better life found fulfillment of their political hopes as part of the general society. Their integration was relatively easy and they often created cultural organizations which allowed them to maintain whatever part of the old homeland they found desirable, although succeeding generations of Jews have worn down the cultural distinctiveness to a large degree. In addition, many have remained interested in causes involving social justice for the general public. In this sense, their political education in Russia made them worthwhile members of the new societies in which they lived.

It is also important to note that those views which appeared utopian and farfetched in Tsarist Russia fared as well as those which appeared mild and based on the continuation of existing social processes. The views of the Zionists fared as well or better than the autonomist and liberal views. In Russia itself the new Soviet regime did not long permit full national expression and returned to a strong assimilationist tendency.

SOME EXTRAPOLATIONS

What does the experience of the Russian Jewish community tell us with respect to other minorities? Granting the uniqueness of any group, experience and conceptualization appear to have great value *per se*. The search for possibilities to improve conditions feeds on itself. The more solutions one finds, the greater the sophistication and the combinations that can be produced. The outcome of such activity is a sharpened sense of opportunity and the greater possibility that it will be put to good use for the minority.

No doubt, giving free rein to imagination appears dangerous, as it did to the conservative forces within Jewish society. The fact remains, however, that those who chose not to act suffered as much as those who did, but the latter found themselves equipped psychologically and in practice to pick up burdens anew and to take the lead whenever circumstances demanded.

Is it not possible that the experience of the old East European Jewish community, the descendant of the Tsarist Russian community, played an important role in the survival of the Jews? The forces which undertook to destroy them or alter their character after 1917 were extremely powerful. But the alternatives available to those who escaped death and adapted themselves to new surroundings allowed the Jews to thwart their enemies by virtue of their experiences, which were the direct results of the Russian Tsarist epoch. To that extent, at least, the Jews made a portion of their history out of that past. Is it not reasonable to ask whether the Jews might have been far greater victims than they were without that experience?

NOTES

1. "Der ershter yidisher sotsialistisher propagandist," *Di Zukunft*, Vol. XXI, No. 11, 1916, 677.

MARCEL RIOUX

QUEBEC

From a Minority Complex
to Majority Behavior

Since the process that the above title encapsulates originates in an ideological shift which took place within the last decade, the following remarks will endeavor to outline the evolution of ideologies in Quebec. For the present purpose, we define ideologies as conceptions that groups have of their identity; this identity is expressed by the definition a group holds of itself and of the other groups with which it interacts. Ethnic and national ideologies are proposed by important subgroups within society and are concerned with the future course of action that the whole ethnic group or nation should follow. Ideologies deal, therefore, with group identity, the goals which the group should pursue and the means to reach them. The dominant class or group within society is the one which succeeds in having its ideology accepted by the other classes and groups. When a society is engaged in an ideological struggle, it means that different groups or classes are fighting to control that society.

This is actually the case in Quebec. Three ideologies are proposed to the French-speaking Québeçois. The dominance of one or the other should settle the fate of that nation for the coming decades. It is far from clear, however, which one will become generally accepted by the population.

39

THE IDEOLOGY OF CONSERVATISM (1840–1945)

In 1534, Jacques Cartier discovered Canada for the King of
France and took possession of it in his name. The beginning of
settlement from France dates back to the beginning of the seventeenth century, when de Mons and Champlain settled in Canada. Champlain founded Quebec in 1608. France held Canada
until 1760, when she lost her to England. It is estimated that
10,000 French colonists came to Canada between 1608 and 1760.
Following the English conquest, most of the members of the
bourgeoisie, the army and the French administration went back
to France. Those who remained were the peasants, the clergy, the
remnants of the bourgeoisie and most of the merchants, traders
and artisans; that group of 65,000 was eventually allowed to preserve most of its culture: language, religion and traditions. The
vast majority of the peasants, which represented the bulk of the
population, continued to till the land in their villages, with their
priests as religious and secular guides. The English administra-
tors and traders elected to live in Montreal and Quebec.

Around 1800, a new French-Canadian elite appeared. Made up
mainly of members of the liberal professions, doctors and lawyers,
it took upon itself to represent the people and to elaborate an
ideology. It defined the French Canadians as a nation which
would eventually gain its political independence under the protection of Britain. With the English minority of Quebec (Lower
Canada), the French-Canadian politicians fought for representative government. The Rebellion of 1837–38 was partly the result
of that struggle. But it was also something else. After the revolt
had been crushed by the English army, Lord Durham presented
his *Report on the Affairs of British North America*. He remarked
that he had come to Canada expecting to find a dispute between
the people and the executive but instead had "found two nations
warring in the bosom of a single state: I found a struggle, not of
principles, but of races." [1]

The remedy he proposed for the ills of Canada was to mark

Quebec for the century to come: it was a blueprint of assimilation. "I entertain no doubt of the national character which must be given to Lower Canada (Quebec); it must be that of the British Empire; it must be that of the great race which must, in the lapse of no long period of time, be predominant over the whole North American Continent. . . . It must henceforth be the first and steady purpose of the British Government to establish an English population, with English laws and language, in this Province, and to trust its government to none but a decidedly English legislature." [2]

The British Parliament passed the Union Act in 1840. It united Lower Canada and Upper Canada (Ontario) into a single state. Until then, the French Canadians were evolving almost normally. Although conquered and dominated politically, socially and economically, they were striving toward eventual independence; they considered themselves a temporarily dominated society but one which looked hopefully to the future. With the Union Act, which amalgamated French Quebec and British Ontario, they lost hope and confidence. They began to see themselves as a minority group whose most vital aim was to preserve its culture. In fighting assimilation and Anglicization, they turned more and more to their past for guidance and inspiration. Their Golden Age lay no more in their future independence but in their French past. To salvage their cultural heritage, they idealized the kind of society they had become. Every trait was to be cherished and preserved. What were the essential traits of that French-Canadian group?

They had become, to survive the first eighty years of British domination, an archaic traditional group living mainly on subsistence agriculture, whose learning was almost exclusively restricted to oral tradition; the birthrate was unequalled by any white population; they were Catholic and French-speaking. The only groups qualified to lead them were their clergy, their doctors and lawyers. These elites elaborated a powerful conservative ideology which was to survive almost intact until the Second World

War. They endeavored to keep the French Canadians agricultural and rural, Catholic and French. Taking advantage of the freedom which the British granted it for its loyalist attitude during the Rebellion of 1837–38, the Church launched a successful counterreformation. In traditional Quebec, doctors and lawyers ("les professionels") made up the upper class, on about the same footing as the clergy. Business men, usually less educated, were not considered as belonging to the same class. It was through politics that "les professionnels" entered the business world and acquired prestige among the English-speaking Canadians and progressively among French-Canadians themselves.

With confederation, in 1867, what had appeared as a menace in 1840, became reality. The French-speaking group of British North America then accounted for about one-third of the population of the Dominion of Canada. Quebec became a province where the French were in the majority. Being a minority in the whole of Canada and dominated economically in Quebec, the French-speaking population adopted the attitude and behavior of a minority group.

The period following confederation marks an economic boom and a period of prosperity for Canada. The dominant economic center passed from Quebec to Ontario, from the east to the center of the country, Canada following in this pattern a North American ecological change. The French-Canadian establishment attempted to counter the displacement of industry by trying to attract more people to agriculture. This move was in keeping with the views of the elites, which had figured that the people would remain Catholic and French only if they lived on farms. Because Quebec lacked industrialization, emigration movements to the industries of New England were amplified, lasting until the end of the century.

When Laurier, a French-Canadian-born lawyer was elected Prime Minister of Canada in 1896, there seemed to be a rapprochement between Quebec and the rest of Canada since he had been elected by both the French- and English-speaking regions of the Dominion. During his term of office, and until 1911, Quebec experienced a significant economic growth. Although Quebec was becoming more industrialized and urbanized, the French-speaking group did not take the initiative in these transformations. It merely supplied labor; capital investments, managers and skilled workers came from other groups—British, Canadian and American.

During the First World War, French Canadians opposed conscription for overseas service, thus reopening the breach between Quebec and the rest of Canada that Laurier had mended. In the postwar period, Quebec continued industrialization with the help of American investments. In 1921, the French-Canadians accounted for only 27.9% of the population of Canada, a decline from previous censuses. The urban population of Quebec was 56.0%; Montreal had 63.9% of French origin.

The beginning of the twentieth century has been marked by the political ideas and action of Henri Bourassa, who belongs as much to Canada as to Quebec. A grandson of Louis-Joseph Papineau, a prominent figure in the 1837–38 Rebellion, Bourassa was active in Quebec and Canadian politics for nearly four decades. This "Red Tory," as Laurier once called him, dreamed of reconciling French-Canadian and Canadian nationalism. The English Canadians, who were then economically and sentimentally linked to the British Empire, were not yet ready for Bourassa's ideas. History shows that on a number of occasions Quebec and English Canada could not synchronize their aspirations. When, at the turn of the century, Bourassa opposed the participation of Canada in the South African War, he started campaigning for an independent Canadian foreign policy disentangled from the imperial British interests. For over forty years, he advocated a kind of pan-Canadian nationalism which, had he been successful, might have more firmly united Quebec and Canada.

But Bourassa was also an ardent French-Canadian nationalist who fought for the cultural rights of his compatriots in both Quebec and Canada. This was the source of dreadful misunderstandings, for his Québeçois compatriots mistook him for a traditional nationalist, even a separatist. Being a devout Catholic and a social conservative, he gave the impression of not differing from the nationalist establishment which had been dominant in Quebec since the Rebellion of 1837–38. On the other hand, he was regarded as an extremist in English Canada, because he urged Canada to sever her links with the British Empire. He opposed the Liberals both in Quebec and at Ottawa, causing the defeat of the government in 1911, then headed by his Quebec compatriot, Laurier. Bourassa exemplified the difficulty of uniting two brands of nationalism. Today, Bourassa's ideas are well accepted in Canada and his Québeçois nationalism, although changed in many ways, is also still alive. But one could conclude that Bourassa's desire for more unity in Canada was unrealized, since Quebec and Canada are no nearer one another today than they were at the beginning of this century.

A political movement advocating the secession of Quebec from the rest of Canada was born during the economic crisis of the 1930's. It was in keeping with traditional nationalism; it aimed at the establishment of a French-speaking, Catholic state whose policies would be modeled on Spanish and Portuguese rightist ideologies. It found a small following in urban centers, among students, intellectuals and petite bourgeoisie.

THE CATCHING-UP IDEOLOGY (1945)

After the Second World War, which resulted in the intensive industrialization and urbanization of Quebec, the ideology of conservatism was seriously contested by various elements of the population who had become fairly important through the years. The domination of the traditional elites, the clergy and the liberal professions, was seriously challenged by union leaders, intellectuals, journalists, artists, students and some liberal-minded members of the old establishment. What was challenged was not the fact that Quebec had a culture (language, religion, traditions) different from the rest of Canada but that that culture should remain unrecognized, as it had been for a century. For the new leaders of opinion, Quebec should catch up with the rest of North America, while preserving its own identity.

According to economists Faucher and Lamontagne: "During the century 1839 to 1939, employment in manufacturing industries in Quebec rose by only a little more than 200,000 . . . Quebec has experienced an employment increase of exactly the same magnitude during only the short space of time between 1939 and 1950. Its relative industrial growth, during these last eleven years, has been ten times as great as it had been during the preceding century and higher than that of Canada as a whole.

"Since 1939, in volume terms, output of manufacturing industries rose by 92 per cent in Quebec and by 88 per cent in Canada, while new investments in manufacturing increased by 181 per cent in this province and by only 154 per cent in the whole country." [3] Quebec has now become the most urbanized province in Canada.

The traditional ideology, which had defined Quebec as agricultural, rural French and Catholic, definitely crumbled under this massive new wave of industrialization and urbanization. However, it was so entrenched in the mentalities and in the political personnel of the Union Nationale, the party in power in Quebec, that this party was defeated electorally just in 1960, which marks the first year of what has been called the Quiet Revolution of Quebec.

Looking back at the period from 1945 to 1960, one could say that the direction of the protest movements was turned inward. Criticism bore mainly against those French Canadians who had allegedly mismanaged the affairs of the province. The traditional elites and their ideology were the favorite targets of the new dissidents. It was after 1960 that the critics turned against what was truly responsible for the socioeconomic domination of Quebec: English-Canadian and American imperialism.

Among the groups which were strongly contested between 1945 and 1960 the clergy was the first target. It was held responsible for the backward educational system and for the general conservative outlook of Quebec during the last century. Criticism developed among progressive Catholics and agnostics who joined together to demand that the clergy withdraw from politics and restrict its activities to religion and the Church. It was a difficult role for the clergy to accept because, since the British conquest in 1760, it had been a guide for the people in both secular and religious matters. For instance, the possessions of the clergy in Quebec were held by some economists to account for one-fourth of the total national wealth of French Canadians.

The second target of the critics was the Union Nationale, headed by the autocrat Maurice Duplessis. He held power all these years by advocating political independence from Ottawa, balanced budgets, and the conservation of the traditional culture of the French Canadians. He was careful to keep the clergy within his influence and managed, with a powerful political machine, to bribe most of the rural districts at election time. He kept attracting foreign capital, mostly American, through tax exemptions and by advertising abroad the "cheap and reliable labor" of the Québeçois.

To defeat Duplessis politically, and the clerical elites ideologically, the opposing forces—union leaders, intellectuals, liberal-minded politicians and the traditional local opposition to the Conservative political regime—had joined forces with the federal Liberal party and campaigned against the alleged backwardness of the political regime and its ideology. Their protest was directed against French Canadians and their activities. Nationalists generally supported Duplessis and the traditional establishment while opposing foreigners, even modern France.

If the opponents of the Duplessis regime knew what they did not wish for Quebec, they hardly took time to outline an ideology to supplant his. It could be inferred from their writings and activities that they favored a strong federal government, free enterprise, "bonne entente" with the non-French elements of the Canadian population, and the establishment in Quebec of a North

American-type of democracy in Canadian politics. One of the most vocal and efficient opponents of Duplessis, Pierre Elliott Trudeau, is now Prime Minister of Canada; a few members of his cabinet, Pelletier, Marchand, Sauvé and Pépin were also vigorous opponents of Duplessis and the conservative ideology during the 1950's. A leading figure of this opposition, Maurice Lamontagne, is also in Ottawa now and sits in the Federal Senate.

THE IDEOLOGY OF

DEVELOPMENT AND PARTICIPATION (1960)

What happened after 1960, the year the Duplessis regime collapsed—Duplessis himself had died the year before—could have been foreseen in the last years of the 1950's. Until that time, it could be said that the French Canadians who were regarded as progressive, socially and economically—Trudeau's type of liberalism—were also antinationalists; those who favored French-Canadian political autonomy were generally conservative in socioeconomic matters. At the end of the 1950's, a new brand of social thought appeared which joined nationalism with a progressive socioeconomic platform. This fact, coupled with the defeat of the Liberals at the federal level, forced provincial Liberals to concentrate on Quebec and outdo Duplessis on his favorite ground: French-Canadian nationalism. To a certain extent, the Liberal forces which defeated the Duplessis regime in 1960 blended nationalism and social democracy. Their slogan was "maîtres chez-nous," meaning that Quebec should be master in her own home.

What could not be foreseen so easily before 1960, is that the Quiet Revolution which developed after 1960 would shake the Québeçois society from top to foundations. The changes envisaged by the Liberal party—government control of education, the nationalization of the electrical resources, the reorganization of the civil service, massive investments in public enterprises, the establishment of public-owned provincial institutions—gave birth to an immense appetite for change. Everything from religion to sex was questioned, and changes generated a craving for more changes.

The most important effect these events had on the Québeçois was to develop a new sense of pride in their own nationality and fatherland. To belong to the French-Canadian group was not viewed as dimly as it was in the 1950's, when Quebec was labeled the only feudal state north of the Rio Grande. The Québeçois soon acquired the knowledge that they could do important things together; they ceased to consider themselves as a minority group within Canada and began to think of themselves as a majority in Quebec and to behave accordingly.

This is the core of the third ideology, which was to develop after 1960. Not only did the Québeçois wish to preserve their cultural heritage, as in the first ideology which dominated for more than a century (from 1840 to 1945), not only did they aspire to catch up economically with the rest of North America, but they began dreaming of establishing a country which would differ from all others in being more democratic, more just and more humane. They began to see themselves as forming not only a minority with a valuable heritage but a modern industrial society which required all the political power necessary to organize its development, as it saw fit. This ideology, besides defining Quebec as a modern industrial society as opposed to a culture, regarded Quebec as underdeveloped and in need of a new type of democracy, to be attained through the participation of all social classes. This view was largely shared by intellectuals and students and, to a lesser extent, by the new middle class—technicians, technocrats and teachers. A new type of nationalism has appeared in Quebec during the last decade.

The sociologist Jacques Brazeau regards the situation as follows: "Many signs show that French Canada's leaders no longer have the orientation of hoping for a return to the past nor feeling satisfied with the maintenance of a small French-speaking aristocracy in Quebec. A new nationalism is growing. It is shared by people who did not belong in the past to sectarian political movements. They seek practical solutions to the problems of French Canada's development, for they believe that the transitional period toward industrial life has lasted long enough." [4]

These new ideas may be seen in the two traditional parties, the Liberal, which came to power in 1960, and among the younger elements of the conservative Union Nationale. Two separatist parties were founded: the R.I.N. (Rassemblement pour l'indépendance nationale) and the R.N. (Ralliement national). Until 1964, the Liberal party continued to effect vast reforms in many areas of Quebec public affairs. Its most important reform was certainly in the educational system. Many observers believe that the magnitude of these reforms caused the defeat of Union Nationale in rural areas in June 1966. The separatist party, the R.I.N., had a few candidates in the Montreal region and drew 9.4% of the votes, causing the defeat of some Liberal candidates. Montreal, the metropolis of Quebec, gave a majority of 53.1% to the Liberals and a mere 30% to the Union Nationale. Most of the rural counties and other regions of Quebec voted for the Union Nationale. The Union Nationale electoral platform was more nationalist than that of the Liberal party during the election in 1966, while the Liberals were more progressive in socioeconomic matters.

In 1967, a few prominent Liberals left their party to found a new political movement which would seek to unify all the separatist movements and gain independence for Quebec. Headed by the dynamic and capable René Lévesque, an ex-Liberal cabinet minister, this movement has gained some momentum lately and is regarded as a threat to both traditional parties. The three ideologies are still fighting one another for supremacy and each has found support in various strata of the population. It is not evident that each political party favors one ideology to the exclusion of the others; like all North American parties, those of Quebec are built more around personalities and interests than ideologies. Inasmuch as party tendencies can be detected, the Union Nationale would appear to be more traditionally oriented and the Liberal party closer to the principles of the American Democratic party. The third ideology finds supporters in both parties and in greater measure among the separatists; it is socialist and future-oriented. Until now, however, there is no important political party in which separatist ideology clearly prevails. The separatists recruit their adherents among students, intellectuals and the new middle classes who, on the whole, share the third ideology.

We stated previously that Quebec and Canada seem unable to desire the same things at the same time. For many decades, Quebec urged Ottawa to accept the idea that Canada is a bilingual, bicultural country, and generations of Quebec nationalists have fought for that principle. But the English Canadians do not seem ready to adopt a policy acknowledging this request. After 1960, when Quebec started her Quiet Revolution, the federal government, seeing that the threat of Quebec's secession was becoming more menacing, set up a royal commission. The purpose of the commission was to investigate bilingualism in Canada and to discover how two cultures respresented in Canada were translated into Canadian institutions and into the daily behavior of people. Published in 1965, the preliminary report of that commission received a cool reception in Quebec because her elites were now more interested in unilingualism in Quebec than in bilingualism in Canada, since Quebec had given up the hope of bilingual recognition. On the other hand, Canada seems to be more favorably disposed towards bilingualism than at any other time in her history.

The various ideologies of Quebec are translated into the labels which the French-speaking group adopts for itself. All through history, the French Canadians have been changing their group names. Before 1840, when the majority of Lower Canada was French-speaking, the appellation was "Canadiens." After 1840, and more especially at Confederation, they were called "French Canadians" by the English Canadians. That name was adopted by the people of Quebec and remained fairly common until 1960, although the peasants had continued to call themselves "Cana-diens." In the 1960's, the name "Québeçois" became more com-mon to designate the inhabitants of the state of Quebec, while "French Canadian" was retained to designate persons belonging to the French-Canadian culture, in Quebec and in Canada. Those who wish the French-speaking people to remain a cultural minority are more apt to use "French Canadiens"; those who ad-vocate more political autonomy or even separation for Quebec, use "Québeçois."

CONCLUSION

In the last decades, Quebec has passed from defining itself as a cultural minority to behaving like a modern nation. It is trying to catch up with the rest of North America and bridge the gaps which have accumulated during the past decades. But the road is not entirely clear. Having developed with American investments, it could hardly keep its present standard of living if it cuts itself away from this capital by adopting drastic economic reforms. There is always the temptation of giving in to Ottawa, which wants to retain its grip on Quebec. It does not seem likely that Quebec will revert to its traditional conservatism, although, if constantly put on the defensive by Ottawa, it could develop con-servative attitudes. It does seem, however, that Quebec is cured of its minority complex.

The June 1968 Canadian election was mainly centered on Quebec. Headed by Pierre-Elliott Trudeau, the Liberal party adopted a firm position against all kinds of Quebec nationalism. It obtained a large majority both in Canada and in Quebec. A majority of English-speaking Canadians voted for Trudeau be-cause they considered that being a French-speaking anti-nationalist Québeçois himself he could make Quebec behave like a minority within Canada and re-assume its traditional role. A majority of French Canadians also voted for Trudeau because since 1896 they have voted for the Liberal party in almost every election. Three times, since Confederation in 1867, the Liberal party chose a French speaking Québeçois as their leader. This policy has helped that party to hold its grip on Quebec.

On the whole, the election of Trudeau last June is interpreted as a setback for Quebec nationalists and separatists and as a repudiation of General de Gaulle's "Vive le Quebec libre." For the present, it seems therefore that the second ideology has increased its chances of becoming dominant in Quebec. It would mean that Quebec would remain within the Confederation and would abandon its aspirations to independence. It is difficult on the basis of what is known of the strength of the opposing social forces to foresee the result of that serious conflict.

NOTES

1. Quoted by Mason Wade in *French Canadians, 1760–1945*, Toronto, 1956, p. 197.

2. *Ibid.*, p. 208.

3. Faucher, Albert and Lamontagne, Maurice: "History of Industrial Development" in Rioux, M. and Martin, Y.: *French-Canadian Society*, vol. I, Toronto, 1965, pp. 258–267.

4. Brazeau, Jacques: "Quebec's Emerging Middle Class" in Rioux, M. and Martin, Y., *French-Canadian Society*, vol. I, Toronto, 1965, p. 327.

FRANCES L. SWADESH

THE ALIANZA MOVEMENT
OF NEW MEXICO
The Interplay of Social Change
and Public Commentary

The most controversial of all the organizations representing
Spanish-speaking people in the United States is the "Alianza"
(Alliance of Free City-States) with headquarters in Albuquerque,
New Mexico. The Alianza has been variously described as a nativistic cult movement (Gonzalez, 1967:71), a criminal conspiracy
(Stang, 1967, 1968) and a movement for social and political
change whose leader, Reies Lopez Tijerina, is its major catalytic
agent: "Whatever happens in the courts to Reies Tijerina, 41,
leader of thousands of poverty-worn Spanish-Americans in
northern New Mexico, he may have been the instrument of social
and political change in the state and he himself may become a
legendary figure" (Ed Meagher, *Los Angeles Times*, 2/5/1968).

The Alianza made front-page headlines in newspapers around
the world on June 5, 1967, when about twenty of its members
raided the Rio Arriba County Courthouse at Tierra Amarilla in
northern New Mexico. They supposedly had intended to make a
"citizen's arrest" of the district attorney, Alfonso Sanchez, on the
grounds that he had illegally arrested some of their fellow Alianza
members and had forcibly prevented the holding of a public
meeting on land-grant demands.

BACKGROUND OF THE LAND GRANT CONTROVERSY

Alianza members are descendants of grantees of lands in New Mexico, Colorado, Arizona, Texas, Utah and California, donated in the seventeenth and eighteenth centuries by the kings of Spain and, from 1822 to 1846, by the Mexican government.

These lands were granted under Castilian laws, exported and adapted to the settlement policies of the New World. In the vast arid lands of what is now the Southwestern United States, volunteer settlers were moved onto lands not occupied by the sparse indigenous population, to live as independent yeoman growing irrigated crops and raising livestock, chiefly sheep.

Under the body of law defining Spanish and Mexican land grants, donations of land could be made to individuals but were more characteristically made to towns or to groups of families desiring to found new communities. Part of each grant was composed of house lots and irrigable lands specifically assigned to individual families. These could be sold by the recipient family or its heirs after the conditions of settlement had been met: building a house, clearing a field, digging an irrigation ditch, growing crops and defending the area from the attacks of nomadic Indians for a period of several years.

By far the largest portion of most grants, however, was the "ejido" (common holding) of the community, which was inalienable and not subject to individual appropriation. Within this category were included irrigated town pastures, usually enclosed, plus the surrounding, unenclosed range and forest lands which, in New Mexico and some other areas, were mountainous and not suitable for agriculture.

Ejido lands throughout Hispanic America have been lost, especially as a market economy began to break down the economic self-sufficiency of subsistence-oriented, traditional, rural communities. The older system of bartering persisted in some underpopulated areas, including northern New Mexico. With the entry of cash transactions, some people inevitably became indebted to others and were forced to pay their debts with their land.

In the United States, however, the loss of the ejido lands on grants was primarily owing to the failure of United States authorities to recognize the ejido principle of land ownership, even though the 1848 Treaty of Guadalupe Hidalgo guaranteed protection of the personal, cultural and property rights of those Mexican citizens who remained north of the newly extended United States border. As a result of this lack of recognition, the grant heirs lost their subsistence base as well as access to such vital resources as timber for fuel and construction and the mineral wealth beneath their former ejido lands. These losses account partially for the fact that more than one-third of all Spanish-speaking families in the Southwest—41% in New Mexico and over 50% in Texas—have incomes below $3,000 per year, a figure which falls well within the designated poverty levels (Samora, 1966: 195).

The central programmatic demand of the Alianza is for a thorough investigation of wholesale violations of the guarantees of the Treaty of Guadalupe Hidalgo. The Alianza claims that these violations have denied personal and cultural rights as well as property rights. This demand has been interpreted in some quarters as a "con game" designed to enrich Reies Tijerina and his associates. In other quarters the Alianza is seen as a standing threat to law and order; and only some observers see the Alianza demands as reasonable premises for negotiations patterned on the Indian Claims cases.

Such contradictory interpretations have affected public opinion on the purposes and leadership of the Alianza. This instability of opinion, in turn, has affected the very pattern of development of the Alianza.

VIEW FROM THE SOUTH

The views expressed in the press of Mexico, which have potential influence upon future developments, are well exemplified by a series of six articles, published in November, 1967, by Manuel

Mejida, a reporter for the Mexico City daily, *Excelsior*. Mejida had toured the Hispano villages of New Mexico and had interviewed many villagers, seeking to enlighten his Mexico City readers on the precipitating causes of the Tierra Amarilla raid.

As a Mexican citizen, Mejida evaluated the land problems of New Mexico from the standpoint of the ejido lands in Mexico. These lands, in substantial areas, had been monopolized by "latifundistas" (plantation owners) who reduced the small farmers to peonage. In the 1930's, a sweeping movement of agrarian reform restored and developed the ejidos in the hands of the communities to which they originally belonged.

Mejida, on the precedent of Mexican experience, considered the grievances of the New Mexicans to be justified. He was impressed by the fact that the land-grant heirs, young and old alike, could state with fair precision the boundaries of their original grants and the acreage which had been appropriated for the public domain, to become, eventually, part of National Forest or state lands, or else to be sold to wealthy Anglo ranchers. Each villager knew the details of who, when, for what purpose and with which consequences areas of their lands had been lost, and each felt the community's loss as a "wound to his own self-esteem" (*Excelsior*, 11/24/67).

Mejida found virtual idolatry among the poverty-stricken villagers for Reies Tijerina, whom they saw as the "incarnation of the justice denied them for one hundred years." Although well-to-do Hispanos tended to see Tijerina and his followers as a "bunch of agitators and bandits," the poor were touchingly confident that, through the Alianza, they could recover their lost subsistence base in the forest and range of their ancestral grants. Some who had been forced to leave the home village to seek livelihood elsewhere expressed hope that their situation was "temporary" and that soon they could return to their traditional life as small independent agriculturalists and stockmen (*Excelsior*, 11/23/67, 11/24/67, 11/25/67).

In view of the violent events of the Tierra Amarilla raid,

Mejida found the villagers surprisingly mild-mannered and free of hatred. Many expressed reluctance to take a stand against their own government for, as Mejida had to remind his Mexico City readers, these were people who valued their United States citizenship, had paid taxes, and served in the Armed Forces without complaint. But they were determined: "We are waiting for the hour of justice . . . never mind how many years our battle for justice takes, we shall win" (*Excelsior*, 11/25/1967).

Women as well as men had devoted vast amounts of time and effort, as well as what little money they had, to the Alianza's cause and they were prepared for more sacrifices in the future. Conversing as individuals or groups, the villagers displayed optimism and determination.

Mejida felt, nonetheless, that he was witnessing "the twilight of Hispanoamerican life in New Mexico." The villages had become so severely depopulated that the Hispano population of New Mexico, long the majority, had sunk below thirty percent in the 1960's. Forced by lack of training (in fields other than farming and livestock) into the ranks of migrant farm labor, many Hispanos had experienced the disruption of community and family life in the process of moving from one state to another in search of jobs. Despite their stubborn loyalty to kin- and community-based values of Hispanic rural culture, the culture was in the grip of disintegrating forces.

Mejida doubted that this poverty-stricken minority group, contemptuously accorded the treatment of a "Beggar's Army," could prevail against the forces of Anglo-dominated wealth and vested interest in confronting their federal government.

Interviewing Governor David Cargo of New Mexico, Mejida found him cautious about gambling his political future on sustained support of the land issues whose validity he acknowledged. Reluctantly, Mejida came to the conclusion that the realities and expediencies of contemporary life in the United States dictate the final extinction of the Hispano way of life in New Mexico (*Excelsior*, 11/27/1967).

DOMINANCE AND THE ETHNOCENTRIC VIEW

Manuel Mejida's melancholy prediction has been voiced for years
by people who eagerly anticipate the extinction of the Hispano
way of life in New Mexico. Crudely stated, their widespread belief is that the Hispanic culture of the Southwest is incurably inferior to the dominant Anglo culture; its language is a broken
patois which must be rapidly forgotten in favor of English; besides, they maintain, the normal fate of all ethnic minority
groups in the United States is to plunge headfirst into the Melt-
ing Pot and come out "Real Americans,"—even if you wouldn't
want your daughter to marry one.

This belief, often operating at deeply unconscious levels of
otherwise informed minds, has tragically affected dominant-
group views of the problems of three groups—the Negro, Indian
and Spanish-speaking people of the United States.

Negroes, in the overwhelming majority, did not voluntarily
come to the United States seeking a better life, but were brought
in chains and subjected to centuries of enslavement followed by
social discrimination and exclusion from the economic opportunities others enjoyed. Indians and Hispanos lived in territories
which were seized by the United States, since which time they
have lived as second-class citizens. Puerto Ricans too became
United States citizens by force of arms. The ideology of the Melt-
ing Pot, therefore, has no basis in reality for these groups.

Dominant-group ethnocentrism has profoundly affected the
political functioning of the above three groups. In the case of the
New Mexicans, this ideology provided the rationale for keeping
New Mexico in the status of a territory long after statehood should
have been granted, with the result that certain semi-colonial characteristics were strengthened and perpetuated to the disadvantage
of the Hispano and Indian populations.

Here is how the editor of the *Harper's Weekly* reacted in 1876
to Senate passage of a statehood bill for New Mexico:

Of the present population, which is variously estimated, and at the last census was 111,000, nine-tenths are Mexicans, Indians, 'greasers', and other non-English-speaking people. About one-tenth or one-eleventh part of the population speak the English language, the nine-tenths are under the strictest Roman Catholic supervision. . . . The proposition of the admission of New Mexico as a State is, that such a population, in such a condition of civilization, of industries, and intelligence, and with such forbidding prospects of speedy improvement or increase—a community almost without the characteristic and indispensable qualities of an American State—shall have a representation in the national Senate as large as New York, and in the House shall be equal to Delaware. It is virtually an ignorant foreign community under the influence of the Roman Church, and neither for the advantage of the Union nor for its own benefit can such an addition to the family of American States be urged. There are objections to a Territorial government, but in this case the Territorial supervision supplies encouragement to the spirit of intelligent progress by making the national authority finally supreme (*Harper's Weekly*, 4/1/1876).

When this diatribe was published, Colorado had already been granted statehood, although its population in 1870 only totalled 39,864 and its mining camps were hardly known for the refinement of their "civilization." By 1910, New Mexico's population had more than tripled, but statehood was delayed another two years. In the interim, the ruling circles of the Anglo minority had formed a partnership with a selected few of the Hispano majority, who were rewarded with material benefits and positions of nominal leadership in exchange for keeping their people under control.

The heritage of this partnership was the characteristic political patronage system of New Mexico, which is often represented as a traditional Hispanic form. In fact, this system overthrew the established democratic forms of Hispanic municipal government, in which the principle of seniority was dominant within a framework of full manhood suffrage, and replaced it with the "paid election," reinforced by threats and promises. By the time New Mexico achieved statehood, the Hispano majority was reduced in ratio and in its capacity to function in its own interest. It had been effectively saddled with a "leadership" that owed its first loyalty to the dominant clique of Anglos.

The Hispano majority managed to impose its will on occasion, for instance, by including in the New Mexico State Constitution a pledge to abide by the terms of the Treaty of Guadalupe Hidalgo. This pledge, however, has been so little honored that it is now widely believed by Anglos that the Treaty and its terms are irrelevant to discussions of the current status of Hispanos.

The descendants of the Spanish-speaking people who became United States citizens under the Treaty, however, believe that its terms are the "supreme law of the land," taking precedence over other laws. They consider the Treaty permanently binding upon *both* signatories. For this reason, the Alianza has, from the beginning, sought to win the active support of the Mexican government to its demand for an investigation into the charges of Treaty violations. The Mexican government, thus far, has avoided taking a position on the matter; on the other hand, the issues involved have stirred widespread popular sympathy when discussed in such press reports as the Mejida series. In Mexico, the New Mexican Hispanos are seen as "the brothers outside."

Such public support might persuade the Mexican government or another government with representation in the United Nations to instruct its delegates to lodge an official request for investigation of possible violation of the Universal Declaration of Human Rights, as the Alianza has been requesting for several years. What is most surprising, in fact, is that New Mexicans have not previously sought a remedy through international channels. Previous failure to utilize means that are nominally available is the result of the lack of political experience and of a genuine political leadership among the Hispanos. Functioning within the existing political structure of New Mexico, Hispanos can only perpetuate their own subordination.

RELATIVE DEPRIVATION
AND THE TACTICS OF DESPAIR

A common line of questioning the intentions and methods of the Alianza begins with the query: Why does the Alianza focus its efforts so sharply on the land question? When it is pointed out that traditional Hispano family and community life depend on a land base, the further questions are raised: Why did the Hispanos wait so long to protest the loss of their lands, and why don't they now seek a remedy through the courts instead of resorting to violence?

Such questions can only be answered by examining the direction of Hispano changes over periods of time, with particular attention to those periods when rapid changes entailing social dislocations have forced groups of Hispanos to action.

The following paragraphs draw upon the author's previous researches (Swadesh, 1964, 1966, 1968) amplified by a series of scholarly articles published in El Dia, a Mexico City daily newspaper, by Agustin Cue Canovas and entitled "The Forgotten People" (Canovas, 1963).

The Canovas articles reviewed the provisions of the Treaty of Guadalupe Hidalgo from the standpoint of maneuvers by the Mexican leadership to protect the rights of its former citizens now incorporated in the United States. Articles 8, 9 and 10 of the Treaty specified the civil and property rights of the transferred citizens, and were ratified by the Mexican government. Article 9 was modified by the United States Senate, but the United States envoys who negotiated the final draft signed a protocol saying that the new wording had the same protective coverage as the earlier draft (Canovas, 5/23/63). Article 10 made provision that all land grants in the territories in question would be "respected as valid and of the stated extension," and that grants whose confirmation had not been completed prior to the United States invasion would be completed or forfeited within a period of two years. The Senate suppressed Article 10 and Canovas surmised that failure to provide for the speedy and automatic confirmation of all valid land grants, as previously pledged, was a prelude to the wholesale and violent expropriations which followed. By failing to specify a procedure and a time period for the confirmation of the grants, Congress set the stage for interminable delays in processing claims, while the Colonial and Mexican Archives were seized and systematically pillaged by the enemies of the grantees (Canovas, 5/23/63, 6/12/63).

The grantees were forced to hire lawyers at their own expense and produce what title papers they could; to go through a lengthy and complex procedure before the Land Commissioner, District Court and Supreme Court; and then seek confirmation by the Surveyor General and, once again, in the Supreme Court. In California, the influx of gold prospectors in 1849 brought about immediate and wholesale violations of the terms of the Treaty; in Texas the picture was even worse.

Mexican authorities protested illegal expropriations, evictions and assassinations, continuing to do so along the Texas border until well into this century, but to no avail (Canovas, 6/12/63). Ironically, President Manuel Peña y Peña, the Mexican president who signed the Treaty of Guadalupe Hidalgo, would have been willing to make even greater territorial concessions to the United States in order to secure the rights of his former fellow-citizens, but he was assured that their freedom was guaranteed and their rights and interests would be protected (Canovas, 10/25/63).

Contrary to the rapid and violent expropriation of grant lands in California and Texas, the same process was more delayed and more veiled in New Mexico. From the time of the arrival of the first New Mexico Surveyor General in 1854 until well after the Civil War, the land-grant heirs presented their claims with little apparent evidence that they would fail to be confirmed. The fact that the overwhelming majority of the population continued to be Hispano masked their growing loss of property and civil rights, for the ejido lands which the surveyor general immediately began to assign to the public domain continued to be unfenced and available for grazing, and the Anglo population was nowhere large enough to present a real threat.

By 1888, however, Antonio Joseph protested to the House of Representatives the situation provoked by denial of statehood to New Mexico. He pointed out that of more than one thousand land-grant claims submitted only 71 had so far been confirmed. Land-grant heirs, despite the Treaty promise to protect them from depredations by nomadic Indian tribesmen, had suffered more than five million dollars' worth of uncompensated damages in the hostilities between the United States and the Navahos and Apaches. Joseph made pointed reference to the distinguished Civil War service rendered by the new citizens from New Mexico (Canovas, 6/24/63).

The protests of Antonio Joseph had little effect. A Court of Private Land Claims was established in 1891 to expedite matters and, when it closed its deliberations in 1904, less than two million acres of land out of thirty-five million acres claimed by the heirs had been confirmed (Read, 1912: 596). Of this acreage, a large portion had remained in the hands of lawyers representing the heirs; for instance, one half the acreage of the Cañon de San Diego Grant (U.S.D.A., 1937: 5–8).

Even so, until grazing lands were fenced off, and the heirs were reduced to their limited agricultural lands, the Hispanos never seem to have recognized the existence of a policy designed systematically to deprive them of their property rights. Each local group, as access was lost, reacted sharply, often with violence, to what they considered an outrage. Starting in the 1880's and continuing to the present, these local groups resorted to vigilante action—cutting fences, burning barns and haystacks and slashing livestock. This was the beginning of the tactics of despair.

During a brief period of years, the ever-deepening impoverish-

ment of the New Mexican Hispano population was relieved by
federal and state programs to restore their economy and meet
their educational needs. In the 1930's, community studies conducted under the Soil Conservation Service of the U.S. Department of Agriculture focused on the relationship between loss of
the subsistence base, land, and social dislocation. In a few communities, direct measures were taken to restore some of the lost
ejido lands to the community. The development of a few stockmen's cooperatives promised to modernize grazing practices
for general community benefit (Loomis and Grisham, 1943). The
Taylor Grazing Act of the 1930's was intended to increase the
grazing lands available to the poverty-stricken communities of
northern New Mexico, but its actual long-term effect has been to
strengthen the domination of corporate livestock interests (see
partial listing of U.S.D.A. publications and Harper et al., 1943:
65).

After this brief respite, the condition of the Hispano villages
took a rapid plunge into deeper impoverishment, as a result of
the wholesale loss of most of their young men to military service
in World War II. When the local population temporarily could
not maintain the livestock industry to the required levels of meat
production for the armed forces, a sharp increase in leasing of
the National Forest range by corporate out-of-state interests took
place, and the villagers have never recovered access to substantial
segments of their traditional range.

Forced emigration from the villages in search of wage work,
which for many years had been a seasonal or temporary means of
meeting subsistence needs for the younger men, now took entire
families away and increased the number of ghost towns in New
Mexico. Between 1950 and 1960, the percentage of New Mexico
Hispanos living in rural communities dropped from nearly 60% to
less than 43% (Samora, 164, Table 2).

While urbanization is a worldwide trend, the cultural shock for
people of a traditional culture, as that involved in such a forced

movement, brings social disaster in its wake. The majority of former villagers who are now obliged to live in the slums of New Mexico's towns and cities constantly express the desire to return to the country, even if they could not hope for better than a marginal subsistence. In large measure, even this thin hope is barred by existing welfare regulations, which deny aid to families owning even the tiniest plot of land which might produce a supplement to their benefits. People forced to go on the welfare rolls, therefore, can only do so after they have sold their land and spent the proceeds.

Comparing life as it is today with what it used to be, forcibly urbanized Hispanos express a keen sense of loss. It is this sense of relative deprivation which is the main motivating force of the Alianza. Even those who have managed to make a livelihood in the city feel that only as small village landholders can they maintain the core values of their culture: the cooperative unity of the enlarged kin group, the firm rules of "respect and honor" handed down from one generation to the next, and the proud sense of their hereditary status, bestowed on them by Philip II, of "hijos-dalgo de solar conocido"—landed gentlemen (Canovas, 7/3/23).

FIRST NOTICE OF THE ALIANZA

Although the Alianza was formally founded on February 2, 1963, Reies Tijerina and his brother Cristobal were in Mexico City early in April, 1962, and the press of the capital ran interviews with the brothers in which they explained their mission.

The Tijerina brothers said that they had come to Mexico City to seek a hearing with the Secretary of Foreign Relations, to request his intervention with United States authorities concerning compliance with the terms of the Treaty of Guadalupe Hidalgo. They explained that for fifty years land-grant heirs had been vainly trying to get recognition of their rights and their lands according to the guarantees of the Treaty. No remedy could be anticipated through the federal district courts because, whenever claims cases had been brought before them, the outcome was pre-determined by those who run the courts—relatives and cronies of the very millionaires who monopolized the lands.

The descendants of land grantees, said the Tijerinas, had asked for United Nations intervention on the grounds of violation of Articles I, III, IV, VII, IX, XV, XXIII and XXV of the Universal Declaration of Human Rights. When Milton Eisenhower, then a delegate to the United Nations, visited Mexico in August, 1959, he had been asked by Dr. Benjamin Laureano Luna, President of the International Front for Human Rights, to intervene on behalf of the petitioners. Despite promises, little had been done because the United States opposed such intervention.

The Tijerinas cited from published works and from recent incidents to illustrate the hardships and discrimination suffered by native New Mexicans who had been penalized by land seizures. Both Hispanos and Indians were included among the examples, for the Pueblo Indian titles to their lands are validated by colonial Spanish documents and the nomadic Indians of the area had a recognized range which was never subjected to permanent settlement prior to the United States occupation. As a matter of fact, Indian claims cases in the Southwest and Rocky Mountain areas have relied on background evidence from the Spanish and Mexican Archives.

One of the cases cited by the Tijerinas as an example of exploitation was the plight of 350 families of heirs to the Sangre de Cristo Grant in southwestern Colorado. In November 1961, a judge had ruled in favor of the claims of a North Carolinian, John Taylor, and had barred the heirs from access to the range and timber of this grant, a right which they had continuously enjoyed until this time. This grant was within the area formerly embraced by New Mexico.

Much emphasis was given in the Mexico City press to the Tijerinas' allegations of denials of cultural rights, in direct violation of the Treaty. The many schools in which children were forbidden to speak Spanish, the constant treatment by Anglos as inferior "foreigners," the reduction of former landowners and independent stockmen to the woeful status of exploited farm laborers toiling in the cotton, tomato and beet fields of the Southwest, were all given as reasons why Hispanos felt robbed and outraged.

The Tijerinas characterized the land-grant heirs as living on the cultural islands of what remained of their land grants in hostile enclavement against the encroaching dominance of the Anglos. Community members who assimilated to Anglo ways were despised as "pochos" (depigmented ones).

Hate, the Tijerinas announced, was growing on both sides. New Mexico papers were announcing with increasing frequency the activities of night riders who attacked Anglo ranches, burned their barns and haystacks and damaged their livestock. In many instances, this was a long-delayed vengeance against the Anglo vigilantes of the 1880's and 1890's who had lynched ancestors of the present heirs.

The Tijerinas expressed their concern that, because no attention had ever been paid to their repeated efforts to gain justice, the Hispanos of New Mexico were becoming so desperate that great violence might suddenly erupt. They urged the Mexican government to intervene on behalf of the descendants of former Mexicans, in order to resolve the crisis.*

These reports, which aroused intense interest in Mexico, did not go altogether unnoticed in New Mexico. The *Albuquerque Tribune,* 9/9/1959, reported the Laureano Luna-Eisenhower interview and commented that the century-old struggle for Southwestern lands whose titles derived from the governments of

---

* The above paragraphs on the April, 1962 Tijerinas' interviews are a summary of articles in *El Tiempo,* 4/4/62, 4/11/62 and 4/12/62 and in *La Prensa,* 4/11/62 and 4/13/62. A more detailed account of the Arizona case was carried in *La Prensa Libre,* another Mexico City daily, on 4/7/63. In this account, it is stated that hundreds of women had appealed to Attorney General Robert Kennedy asking his help to obtain observance of the Treaty of Guadalupe Hidalgo. In none of these accounts was the name of the community mentioned —"City of Peace"—nor the fact that the Tijerinas had been among the victims of depredations.

Spain and Mexico had now been reopened as a historic international issue.

EMERGENCE OF THE ALIANZA

Shortly after the founding meeting of the Alianza, on February 2, 1963, Reies Tijerina wrote a letter to the Mexico City daily, *El Dia,* outlining the current situation as he saw it. He wrote that as many as ten million heirs might have a stake in the drive that was about to reopen all 1,715 land grant claims in the Southwest.*

In his letter, Tijerina compared the lot of dispossessed land-grant heirs to that of people in underdeveloped countries. Forced into the migrant labor stream, many were precluded from earning an adequate family livelihood and, as an alternative to starvation, became permanently dependent upon surplus commodities handed out by the government.

Tijerina reiterated the appeal of land-grant heirs to the Mexican government to investigate the Treaty violations in the light of complaints and historical documents which had been assembled: "For five years, we have been telling the Mexican people and the whole world about our pressing problems, which are really based on the drive to take away all our grants." Tijerina expressed confidence in the genuine concern Mexican people felt for this issue, and added for their information that U.S. Secretary of the Interior Stewart Udall had recently voiced objections to widespread land frauds and robbery (*El Dia,* 4/21/1963).

---

* The 1960 "Spanish-surname" population for the five states of New Mexico, Colorado, Arizona, Texas and California has been given as about four million, of whom some half million are of Mexican parentage. Such estimates are admitted to be subject to correction and, for the country at large, estimating the Hispanic population becomes largely guesswork. This is because the children of non-Spanish-surname fathers and the wives of non-Spanish-surname husbands, regardless of their own Hispanic descent and affiliation, are placed in other categories. Some people anglicize their surnames in order to "pass." Some Mexican nationals slip across the border each year without registering. Finally, if we include among Tijerina's ten million potential claimants those Mexican nationals whose ancestors fled New Mexico after

Within a month, *El Dia* responded to the Tijerina letter by running the Agustin Cue Canovas series. This entire series was reprinted in the original Spanish by the alert editor of the *Albuquerque News-Chieftain,* starting on September 7, 1963. Nigel Hey, editor of the *News-Chieftain* at that time, early recognized the public interest and potential significance of the Alianza cause. For more than two years, he provided space for a weekly column by Reies Tijerina, written in Spanish and widely discussed among Spanish-speaking people. The Spanish-broadcast radio station KABQ also provided time for daily talks by Tijerina. As a result, a high level of awareness concerning land-grant issues grew among the Hispanos of Albuquerque, while the information remained largely unknown to the monolingual Anglo population.

Nigel Hey also covered the first annual convention of the Alianza. It was held on September 1, 1963, in the Rio Grande High School gymnasium. Representatives of about fifty land grants attended. The main discussion concerned the building of a central mutual-aid group for all land-grant heirs in the Southwest. They would pool their efforts, employ the best attorneys and bring political pressure to bear in Washington in order to obtain redress. Another highlight of the convention was a report on Reies Tijerina's recent trip to Washington to enlist the aid of the attorney general on the land-grant issue. On the same trip, Tijerina had attended the American Emancipation Centennial in Chicago and had invited its Negro president, Dr. Alton Davis, to be keynote speaker at the Alianza convention. Mexico's former president, Miguel Alemán, had been a speaker at the centennial and had expressed interest in the land-grant struggle (*Albuquerque News-Chieftain,* 9/7/63).

The 1962 interviews in the Mexico City press had touched on the parallels which Tijerina saw between the Negro struggle for

---

1846, a group of large but undetermined numbers in the northern states of Mexico, it is possible that his estimate is reasonably accurate.

liberation and equality and that of New Mexico's Hispanos as well as the entire "raza" (all New World, Spanish-speaking peoples, regardless of racial antecedents). Tijerina had also expressed his view that a special relationship of long duration and much intimacy existed between Indians and Spanish-speaking people of the Southwest. Although he held that each group had its special problems and methods of struggle, he actively sought understandings with Indian leadership and urged his members to learn from the Negro struggle.

Tijerina's inter-ethnic outlook and strategy was as much of an innovation at the first annual convention of the Alianza as was his proposal to link the fortunes of all grants into one major drive in which property rights and civil and cultural rights were seen as indivisible. It is remarkable that both the outlook and the proposal were so readily adopted by the bulk of the Alianza membership, considering their lack of previous exposure to broadly based, politically oriented movements and also considering the frequently voiced condemnation by middle-class Hispanos of this adoption of "Negro tactics" and "loss of traditional Spanish dignity" (see the Spanish-language "Poco a Poco" column in the *Española New Mexican*, 7/21/66, for a characteristic statement along these lines).

As reported in the press of both Mexico and New Mexico, 1964 was a year of intensive organizing activities for the Alianza, spurred by an April delegation to Washington to lay their problems before congressmen. According to the *Albuquerque Tribune*, "Rep. Montoya said he has given his assurance that he will support any legal means that might be found within the existing legal framework to resolve title conflicts" (7/30/1964). Montoya was asked to introduce a bill for a congressional investigation into the heirs' complaints and claims, which representatives Roybal of California and Gonzales of Texas promised to support once it was initiated.

In 1964, tensions were mounting on the Tierra Amarilla Grant. The grant heirs were posting signs ordering all people lacking an heirship claim to the grant land to vacate. A plaintive letter from a Tierra Amarilla resident indicated the state of mind of the heirs. "Some of us are pretty desperate. We have tried to be good citizens and our reward has been no justice in the courts and powdered milk from the Welfare. We don't want Welfare, we want enough of our land to graze a milk cow." The same writer asked how it was possible for the United States to enforce to the hilt the treaties that gave it the Canal Zone and Guantanamo Base, yet to ignore its own obligations in the Treaty of Guadalupe Hidalgo (*Albuquerque Journal*, 7/1964).

ATTENTION FROM LAWMEN

On February 13, 1964, *El Mexicano*, a Ciudad Juarez daily, published an interview with Reies Tijerina concerning a proposed motorcade of land-grant heirs from Albuquerque to Mexico City. They wanted to bring their demands to the attention of the people and governments on both sides of the border. Tijerina cited the Laws of the Indies and the 1493 Papal Bull "Noverunt Universi," establishing a policy for colonization of the New World. These laws had set the basis of land ownership which the United States had pledged to respect in the Treaty of Guadalupe Hidalgo and Tijerina pointed out that it was the duty of both signatories to the Treaty to see that it was upheld.

When Tijerina went to map the route of the caravan, however, he was arrested by agents of the Judicial Police and held in the Chihuahua State Prison, pending a decision on his status by the Secretariat of Gobernacion (which controls travel and immigration in Mexico). The shock and anger which this abrupt and unexplained action aroused throughout Mexico, where festivities for the New Mexico pilgrims were being planned, was reflected in the news report of the Chihuahua City publication *Accion* (7/15 /1964).

Secretary Diaz Ordaz of the Gobernacion, who has since become the president of Mexico, allowed Tijerina to be released from prison and to proceed to Mexico City, where he was suddenly rounded up and deported. Ironically, while all this was going on, Governor Campbell of New Mexico announced that he would provide a police escort for the motorcade to the Texas border (*Albuquerque Tribune*, 7/30/1964). News of the arrest had not yet come to New Mexico. In 1967, Mexican journalist Eduardo Septrien reminisced that New Mexico Hispanos had been thunderstruck by the arrest and deportation of their leader, since they had never dreamed that the country of their forefathers might one day reject them (n.d.).

THE ALIANZA GROWS

When the second annual convention of the Alianza took place in Seth Hall, Santa Fe, on August 28–29, 1964, its membership was claimed to be 6,000 (*Albuquerque North Valley News*, 8/27/1964); by 1966 the number had risen to 20,000 (*Denver Post*, 4/25/1966). The early growth of the Alianza was no doubt spurred by hopes that Joseph Montoya, now a senator, would sponsor a bill for an investigation of land-grant grievances. In mid-1965, however, Reies Tijerina announced in his weekly *News-Chieftain* column that neither Montoya nor the President, who had received many appeals, appeared to be concerned about the problems of the land-grant heirs. Tijerina began to discuss the possibility of bringing the issue of the Treaty directly before the Supreme Court (*Albuquerque News-Chieftain*, 8/6/1965).

The third annual convention of the Alianza, held on September 4–5, 1965, voted to assess each member family $100 in order to create a legal action fund. A New Mexico attorney and one from Texas were retained to study procedures aimed at opening up the question of vacant lands taken from the grants by either the state or federal government. By January, 1966, the heirs had managed to raise $5,000 but it became increasingly apparent that vastly larger sums would be needed to launch such a case (*Albuquerque Journal*, 1/1/1966).

At this time, Tijerina began to consider laying the groundwork for a litigation in which the Alianza would be the defendant and would thereby be spared the high cost of going to court as plaintiff. By acts of civil disobedience on grant lands which had been taken by the federal government, the Alianza could challenge the government to prove that these lands were, indeed, its rightful property.

Other kinds of acts of civil disobedience had already been committed by land-grant heirs. For example, members of the "Abiquiu Corporation" of the Tierra Amarilla Grant, were accused by District Attorney Alfonso Sanchez of violating a 1964 court injunction forbidding them to issue hunting, grazing and fishing permits to people who were not grant heirs. In the citation, Sanchez stated: "The Alianza Federal de Mercedes and Reies Lopez Tijerina are the primary instigators and advisors to the remaining defendants in the unlawful acts herein complained of" (*New Mexican*, 1/5/1966). Mr. Sanchez gave no factual basis for this allegation.

Another case of civil disobedience which became linked in the popular mind with the Alianza led to the filing of criminal charges by District Attorney Sanchez in the fall of 1966 against the parents of twenty-five primary-school children of the town of Cañones, a remote hamlet of northern New Mexico. The parents had refused to send their children to school in Coyote, over twenty miles away, on the grounds that the road out of Cañones became too dangerous in rainy or snowy weather. It was generally felt that the parents were also protesting the closing of the Cañones school which caused the transfer to Coyote. The parents disavowed ties with the Alianza (*Albuquerque Journal*, 10/6/1966).

While it is quite possible that the parents were acting on their own, it is equally possible that issues raised by the Alianza served as a stimulus to their actions. But the Alianza was beginning to launch a different kind of struggle as its central educational demand: to assert the right of Hispano children to use their own language in school. Tijerina told reporter Peter Kelly that recovery of lands was simply a part and, to an extent, a symbol of the full purpose of the Alianza, which was to mold an effective, influential organization of Hispanos, united in culture, language and pride of identity. In his vivid, nonidiomatic English, Tijerina pictured the suffering and alienation experienced by Hispano children in school: "Culture is a live part of people. All language of ours has been deprived from public schools. Our children feel there's no future in education. They have no zeal. Cultural ties become our chains" (*Denver Post*, 4/25/1966).

While pondering the implementation of acts of civil disobedience, the Alianza made one last effort to secure justice through congressional action. A march to Santa Fe was undertaken during the Fourth of July holiday to ask Governor Campbell's assistance in pushing for a Congressional bill. This was the Alianza's first, mass, direct action, and for many Alianza members it was the first demonstrative public action of their lives. Reaction to the demonstration was vocal, some highly critical. Dr. Nancie Gonzalez of the University of New Mexico Department of Anthropology probably expressed the dominant reaction, however, when she predicted to an *Albuquerque Journal* reporter that there would be "more ferment as this American discovers and raises his Spanish-speaking voice" (7/3/1966).

The fourth annual convention of the Alianza, held September 3–4, 1966, demonstrated the growth of interests among the members in topics ranging far beyond the Laws of the Indies and the Treaty of Guadalupe Hidalgo, which some observers tended to view as obsessional concerns. Much interest was registered in such topics as language discrimination and de facto segregation in the schools, the virtues and defects of poverty programs, and the war in Vietnam, with its high death toll among Spanish-surname soldiers (*Albuquerque Journal*, 9/3/66).

In October, 1966, the Alianza members occupied the Echo Amphitheater Campground in the Carson National Forest, a site in northern New Mexico which was on the 500,000 acre San Joaquin del Cañon de Chama Grant. The purpose of the occupation, as stated by Mrs. Isabel Garcia at the trial which resulted one year

later, was to get the land-grant issue into the courts: "The purpose
was that we would go to the Echo Amphitheater and if we were
arrested, we would get our case in court and maybe go to the Supreme Court." Deliberate mass exposure to arrest had been voted
by the membership and was approved by the Supreme Council of
the Alianza, a group of twelve "older, more experienced men,"
according to Mrs. Garcia (*Alamogordo Daily News,* 11/9/1967).

PROS AND CONS

During the occupation of the Echo Amphitheater Campground,
the Santa Fe *New Mexican* (10/27/66) ran an editorial entitled
"Not a Laughing Matter," which reflected the rising tide of
public support for a thorough study of the land-grant question. It
said in part:

> We can't laugh because our conscience is pricked . . . mor-
> ally the case is far less clear . . . behind the legal technicali-
> ties we are confronted with the shameful fact that the United
> States of America made a solemn promise and failed, in
> many instances, to honor the obligations of that promise.
> People who were guaranteed the perpetual (and often tax-
> free) right to the use of ancestral lands have lost that right
> and the United States, which assumed an obligation to pro-
> tect them, did nothing to honor its pledge. . . . Land Grant
> heirs are asking that a federal commission investigate this
> situation and right the old injustice. Whatever the technical-
> ities of the law, we think the national conscience would rest
> easier if this were done.

The Forest Service attempted to dampen support by alleging
that a Chama Cañon Grant of the size claimed by the heirs had
never existed. In 1894, the Rio Grande Land and Cattle Company, headed by Thomas Burns, had indeed laid claim to a grant
of this name, alleging that it consisted of some 500,000 acres.
Upon investigation, the Court of Private Land Claims, found the
grant consisted of only 1,422 acres. This finding was confirmed

by the Supreme Court in 1897. The grant was confirmed to legal heirs, and still exists as a small enclave within the Carson National Forest (*New Mexican*, 10/30/1966).

The Forest Service neglected to mention later litigation on the Chama Cañon Grant which tends to vindicate the Alianza claim. A fresh suit for the full half-million acres was entered by attorney Thomas B. Catron on behalf of the Rio Arriba Land and Cattle Company in 1898, and Thomas Burns received patent on the entire grant minus the 1,422 acres in 1905. Mr. Burns did not hold this grant for long because it lay within the area which soon became the central section of the Carson National Forest (Cañon de Chama Grant, Reel 20, New Mexico Land Grant Microfilm Series).

SHOCK WAVES

The June 5, 1967 raid on the Tierra Amarilla courthouse alienated some Anglo opinion but obviously aroused enthusiasm and downright pride among wide sections of the Hispano population. A number of research-oriented articles appeared in the press, probing into the underlying causes of the raid. Few of these articles were as sympathetic toward Alianza members as the aforementioned Mejida articles in *Excelsior;* on the other hand, emphasis was laid on the existence of justified grievances.

The Las Cruces trial, held in early November, 1967, received fair and restrained press coverage in all parts of the country. Although the prosecution made much of holding the two forest rangers for an informal "trial" during the occupation of the Echo Amphitheater Campground, and described the temporary confiscation of their trucks and radios as "seizure of government property," a number of the reporters paid more attention to the implications of social change among the New Mexico Hispanos which were revealed through the trial.

On November 9, 1967, the *Sun-News* of Las Cruces summed up the testimony of Reies Tijerina as follows:

While explaining his aims, Tijerina claimed that the U.S. Supreme Court and Court of Appeals have consistently ruled that the courts do not have jurisdiction over political matters or entities such as the pueblos his groups claim. He explained that his group is striving to 'build up moral strength' to give its case validity in the courts. . . . 'The law means only what people behind it mean,' Tijerina declared. He explained that judges follow an established pattern in court and that his group is working to adjust that established way of looking at the law.

Ed Meagher of the *Los Angeles Times* summarized an account of the Tijerina testimony in which the drive for civil and cultural rights was stressed: "The economic, political and social rights questions raised by the Spanish-American movement have New Mexico in a turmoil" (11/20/1967).

ATTACK FROM THE RIGHT

In October, 1967, a pamphlet was issued by *American Opinion*, a publication of the John Birch Society, entitled "Reies Tijerina— the Communist Plan to Grab the Southwest." The pamphlet came out in time to be widely circulated just before the trial in Las Cruces, and rumor has it that some 50,000 free copies were distributed within the area from which the jury was soon to be drawn. However this may be, the pamphlet's author, Alan Stang, made a number of speeches along the lines of the pamphlet in various communities in New Mexico, both before and during the trial.

Defense attorneys for the five defendants in the Echo Amphitheater Campground case considered the pamphlet so prejudicial to their clients that they asked that the trial be moved out of New Mexico altogether. "The John Birch Society is now attempting to smear the land grant movement as a Marxist revolutionary cabal," stated the attorneys, as they deposited along with their motion sixteen exhibits, consisting of newspaper clippings and comment by radio stations (Santa Fe *New Mexican*, 10/21/1967).

In March, 1968, *American Opinion* published a second Stang pamphlet entitled "Terror Grows—'War on Poverty' Supports Castroite Terrorists." This was Stang's "exposé" of the "links" between the Alianza and employees of the New Mexico State Office of Economic Opportunity.

The speedy effect of the Stang pamphlets and the investigation into "possible Tijerina-Red links" which the State Attorney General ordered in the fall of 1967 (*Albuquerque Tribune*, 9/12/1967) was to cool the interest of those individuals who had hoped to reap political advantage by basking in the reflected glow of the Alianza's growing popularity. Another effect was to usher in a period of increasingly harsh treatment of Alianza members, which was justified in newspaper editorials.

On the night of January 2, 1968, the Tierra Amarilla jailor, Eulogio Salazar, who was to have been a key witness in the raid case, was brutally bludgeoned to death. Cristobal Tijerina and another Alianza member, Felix Martinez, were arrested the following day. Although it rapidly became apparent that they could not have been guilty of the crime, and no guilt could be attached to any Alianza member, Governor Cargo recommended cancellation of bond for seventeen other defendants in the raid case. Many were forced to spend more than a month in prison, yet to this day the Salazar case remains unsolved.

A January 6, 1968 editorial in the *Albuquerque Journal*, signed by editor John McMillion stated: "If not directly involved the Alianza is indirectly involved because it has nurtured such hate as never before existed in Rio Arriba County." McMillion warned the citizens of the area that "while they may have been shortchanged in the past they certainly will be denied even more in the future if the community, and the area, becomes a fiefdom run by hoodlums."

When the preliminary hearing on the Tierra Amarilla raid took place in early February, 1968, signs stating "Tierra o

Muerte" (Land or Death) appeared on fenceposts of the Tierra
Amarilla Grant. Without pausing to learn that this was the traditional slogan of the followers of Emiliano Zapata during the
Mexican Revolution, one paper termed it an "ominous warning"
(*Clovis Journal,* 2/11/1968) and another described a "drawing of
a Pancho Villa-type Mexican bandit with a bandolier of ammu-
nition across his chest" (*Rio Grande Sun,* 2/8/1968).

The most hostile editorial attack occurred when the preliminary hearing on the raid ended with charges against nine of the
defendants dismissed and, those against the remaining eleven
defendants greatly reduced. The editor of the *Albuquerque Tribune,* George Carmack, wrote an open letter to his readers on February 10. He demanded that preliminary court hearings in criminal cases be replaced by the Grand Jury system. District Attorney
Alfonso Sanchez, who was bitterly critical of the judge's rulings,
promptly called a meeting of the Rio Arriba County Grand Jury.
The consequent Grand Jury indictment restored all the charges
eliminated or reduced by the judge (*Albuquerque Journal,* 4/28
/1968).

Nothing further was mentioned about the social-change role of
the Alianza, the grievances it sought to redress and the success of
its organizing efforts. Then on February 14, 1968, Santa Fe *New
Mexican* reporter Peter Nabokov managed to interview Reies Tijerina between his release from prison and his departure on a
fund-raising tour of California. Tijerina was hoping for help in
this campaign from César Chavez, leader of the farm workers;
from Bert Corona, head of the Mexican-American Political Association; and from a number of other well-known West Coast
leaders. He also discussed the preparation of the Alianza's claims
for presentation before the United Nations.

POOR PEOPLE'S MARCH

The New Mexico public, saturated with the bloody details of the
Salazar slaying and the preliminary hearing on the Tierra Amarilla raid, was startled to learn in April, 1968, that Reies Tijerina

had been the personal choice of Dr. Martin Luther King to coor-
dinate the New Mexico section of the Poor People's March. King
also chose him to be a principal leader of the entire Southwest
contingent. Under the title "Tijerina: the Wrong Choice," the
Albuquerque Journal editorialized concerning "Tijerina's record
. . . marked by violence." Itemizing every instance in which the
Alianza had been involved in violent episodes, including the Salazar murder and the dynamiting of the Alianza headquarters by
a saboteur who clumsily blew off his own hand, the editorial concluded: "Tijerina's presence seems almost certain to lessen the
prospects that the march will be a non-violent one" (3/2/1968).

Expressions of this sort brought forth abundant anti-Tijerina
statements, all of which were duly relayed to the organizing staff
of the Southern Christian Leadership Conference. Despite ensu-
ing misunderstandings, blunders, harsh words and harsher feelings, the New Mexico contingent did leave with Tijerina at its
helm.

ASSESSMENT AND PROGNOSIS

With the Poor People's campaign, the Alianza entered a new and
complex phase of its development. Assessments of its promise
vary. Paul Wieck of the *Albuquerque Journal* was negatively
impressed by Tijerina's disagreements with the SCLC leadership
and felt that they largely arose because he "didn't get his cut of
the cash." Wieck also objected to Tijerina's statement that the
SCLC leadership had betrayed the land-reform goals of the campaign. Wieck concluded that "Tijerina, as a spokesman for a
land based movement, has little to offer the more sophisticated
men in SCLC and other civil rights organizations" (*Albuquerque
Journal*, 7/15/1968).

Paul Wieck apparently forgot that Dr. King had emphasized
his intention to link land demands of the former sharecroppers of
the Deep South, who have in recent years been displaced by machine operations and who represent the most critically dislocated
element forced into the urban ghettoes, with the Hispano and

Indian demands. Whereas the Hispano and Indian claims derive from treaties, the Negro claim is based on the post-Civil War promise of "forty acres and a mule" for every freedman.

Faith Berry, a Negro free-lance writer who spent a good deal of time at both the Washington, D. C., Resurrection City and at headquarters at the Hawthorne School, where the Spanish-speaking delegation had its headquarters in Washington, gave a different picture from that presented by Paul Wieck. She found that rifts between the SCLC leadership and the leaders of the Indian and Hispano ethnic groups occurred because the latter objected to "being handed final decisions on policy by the Southern Christian Leadership Conference," instead of being directly represented in policy making.

Miss Berry was greatly impressed by the growth of inter-ethnic dialogue which had become a feature of life at the Hawthorne School and which involved youths from all groups, including the whites from Appalachia. She felt that Hispano initiative had launched this significant development, which might well turn out to be the most enduring achievement of the entire campaign.

Miss Berry quoted Tijerina as follows:

> We need unity. This is the first opportunity the poor and deprived of this country have had to come together. But some of our goals and demands are different. We Spanish-Americans put emphasis on our treaty because for us the treaty would settle the issue for many of us for jobs, food, discrimination, education and the improvement of our rural areas. In the cities of the Southwest, we are discriminated against just like the black man, but like the black man we are learning to fight back (*New York Times Magazine,* 7/7/1968).

Retracing the development of the Alianza from a small, isolated group of tradition-oriented Hispanos through its brief and stormy years, one hesitates to predict the future dimensions of this organization and the areas of its emphasis. From the start, it has disregarded all the rules for developing an organization, and has never thrived more than when apparently on the brink of failure. In the absence of any other effective Hispano organization in New Mexico devoted to social change, the Alianza has taken on an unwieldy program that puts it in the position of having to learn many things very fast, both in the field of practical politics and in statesmanlike advancement of proposals for economic betterment, education and the like.

Yet, in these formidable tasks, the Alianza can now draw upon a wide reserve of interested allies, who are learning as much from rural Hispanos as they are teaching them. The author is convinced that the Alianza movement is developing in accordance with the classic form of innovative movements in conflict situations with revolutionary overtones:

> While a great deal of doctrine in every moment (and, indeed, in every person's mazeway) is extremely unrealistic in that predictions of events made on the basis of its assumptions will prove to be more or less in error, there is only one sphere of behavior in which such error is fatal to the success of the revitalization movement: prediction of the outcome of conflict situations. If the organization cannot predict successfully the consequences of its own moves and of its opponents' moves in a power struggle, its demise is very likely. If, on the other hand, it is canny about conflict, or if the amount of resistance is low, it can be extremely 'unrealistic' or extremely unconventional in other matters without running much risk of early collapse (Wallace, 1956:279).

Today, with great emphasis, the minority groups are joining together to demand that the majority group speedily shed itself of racism, ethnocentrism and the propensity to control "lesser" peoples by means of violence. Representatives of the majority group cannot agree whether to meet those demands with tactics of repression and terror, with token concessions or with full compliance. Considering the fears, guilty consciences and indecisions that plague so many majority group Americans and the growing experience, self-confidence and unity which increasingly unites the discriminated and dispossessed, the larger movement of which the Alianza is an integral part can hardly fail.

NOTES

Canovas, Agustin Cue
1963 El Pueblo Ovidado, series in *El Dia,* daily newspaper of Mexico City
5/23/1963, 5/29/1963, 6/12/1963, 7/3/1963, 6/no date/1963, 6/20/1963, 6/24/1963, 7/10/1963, 10/4/1963, 10/10/1963, 8/1/1963, 8/29/1963, 10/25/1963, 10/30/1963
Gonzalez, Nancie L.
1967 The Spanish American of New Mexico: A Distinctive Heritage
Advance Report #9, Mexican-American Study Project,
Los Angeles: University of California Graduate School of Business Administration
Harper, Allen G., Cordova, Andrew and Oberg, Kalervo
1943 Man and Resources in the Middle Rio Grande Valley,
Inter-American Studies, II,
Albuquerque: University of New Mexico Press
Loomis, C. P. and Grisham, Glen
1943 "Spanish Americans: The New Mexico Experiment in Village Rehabilitation," *Applied Anthropology,* 2(3): 13–37
Meagher, Ed
1967 "Tijerina Forays Seen as Civil Rights Struggle,"
Los Angeles Times, 11/20/1967
1968 "Tijerina Raid May Bring Social Change,"
Los Angeles Times, 2/5/1968
Mejida, Manuel
1967 Series in *Excelsior,* a daily newspaper of Mexico City
El Problema Moreno, 11/23/1967
Fantasmas Junto al Rio Bravo, 11/24/1967
Ejercito de los Desarrapados, 11/25/1967
Ocaso de los Hispanoamericanos, 11/27/1967
Read, Benjamin
1912 *Illustrated History of New Mexico,*
Santa Fe: Sante Fe New Mexico Printing Company
Samora, Julian, ed.
1966 *La Raza: Forgotten Americans,*
Notre Dame: University of Notre Dame Press

Septrien, Eduardo
1967 n.p.d.
      ¿ Guerrillas en los Estados Unidos?
Stang, Alan
1967 "Reies Tijerina—The Communist Plan to Grab the Southwest,"
      Belmont, Massachusetts: *American Opinion*
1968 "Terror Grows—'War on Poverty' Supports Castroite Terrorists,"
      Belmont, Massachusetts: *American Opinion*
Swadesh, Frances L.
1965 "Property and Kinship in Northern New Mexico,"
      Rocky Mountain Social Science Journal, 2/1: 209–214
1966 "Hispanic Americans of the Ute Frontier,"
      Unpublished Ph. D. Dissertation, University of Colorado
      (Research Report #50, Tri-Ethnic Project)
1968 "The Alianza Movement: Catalyst For Social Change,"
      Text of a Report Delivered at the Annual Meeting of the American
      Ethnological Society, Detroit, Michigan, May 5, 1968.
      To be published in Proceedings of the Annual 1968 Spring Meeting
      of the American Ethnological Society (Fall, 1968)
United States Department of Agriculture, Soil Conservation Service,
Regional Studies
1936 Reconnaissance Survey of Human Dependency on Resources in the
      Rio Grande Watershed,
      Regional Bulletin #33
1937 Notes on Community-Owned Land Grants in New Mexico,
      Regional Bulletin #48
1939 Tewa Basin Study, Vol. 2. The Spanish-American Villages,
      Office of Indian Affairs Land Research Unit, 1935.
      Released by United States Soil Conservation Service, Region 8,
      Albuquerque, New Mexico
Wallace, Anthony F.C.
1956 "Revitalization Movements," *American Anthropologist*, 58: 264–283

N.B. I am indebted to leaders of the Alianza for lending me their press
file. Unfortunately, some of the clippings are without dates, name of publication or even title of article. Particularly for some of the Mexican press clippings, these deficiencies cannot be remedied.

SUZANNE L. SIMONS

THE CULTURAL AND SOCIAL SURVIVAL OF A PUEBLO INDIAN COMMUNITY*

Examination of minority group responses to a larger society involves economic, political, social, and ideological dimensions. Given a hypothetical continuum of change or adaptation to outside pressure, minority groups may be classified at the extremes as (1) those which have changed little or not at all and, at the opposite end, (2) those which have radically altered in these respects. The middle of the continuum would comprise a multiplicity of minority groups which exhibit varying degrees of change in one or more of the dimensions.

To make such a classification meaningful, however, it is necessary to describe the types of change made in these dimensions, whether towards closer approximation to the values of the larger society; further intensification of what already exists within the minority group; or some kind of transformation in which elements of the larger society and elements of the minority group take on a distinctive configuration.

In addition, it is essential to explore the conditions within the minority group society which contribute to the maintenance or change of traditional elements. This is primarily a matter of the degree of existing solidarity and the mechanisms extant for its

* The field work for this paper was subsidized by the American Association of University Women (AAUW), the National Science Foundation (NSF) and the Public Health Service (PHS).

continuation in the face of outside pressure. In short, examination of minority group responses to a larger society involves investigation of what has changed or been perpetuated, how this has been accomplished, and why the responses have been facilitated.

The following account explores the reactions of one small Indian community to the larger American society in light of these considerations. It will be apparent to the reader that change has been more extensive in some dimensions than in others and that the processes of assimilation, intensification, and transformation have resulted in a highly complex response. The reader is urged to note the essentially inward nature of community activities and interests and the structural and ideological mechanisms which foster it. Undoubtedly the fact that this minority group is territorially contained provides a special set of conditions for perpetuating its identification which many other minority groups lack.

The community in question is that of the Sandia Indians, who live in a small community located approximately 15 miles north of Albuquerque, New Mexico, and a few miles south of the town of Bernalillo, New Mexico. When the Spaniards explored this Rio Grande River area in the sixteenth century, they found Sandia to be a well-settled community of approximately 4000 inhabitants, who practiced a horticultural way of life on land adjoining the nearby river. Under Spanish conquest, the Sandias adopted livestock raising, fruit cultivation, and new crops such as wheat. In addition to subsistence changes, the Spaniards introduced Catholicism, features of which exist today alongside the traditional religion, and superimposed civil government to function along with the older theocratic system.

At the end of the seventeenth century, Indian hostility toward the Spaniards led to a general uprising. Most of the Sandias fled westward, establishing themselves among the Hopi. Greatly decimated, some of the refugees and their descendants returned to their ancestral land about fifty years later, resuming their horticultural and livestock-raising activities.

The pueblo remained under Spanish control until the territory of New Mexico was ceded to the United States in the nineteenth century. By United States-Spanish agreement, the Sandia land grant originally recognized by the Spaniards continued to be honored by the United States government. A portion of the grant has since passed into the hands of the United States government or its citizens. Some of the western slope of the Sandia mountain was purchased by the government at the beginning of this century. Other land passed into private hands through purchase or transfer, at a time when Indian land rights were less protected than today.

The population of Sandia was greatly reduced at the beginning of this century by a plague still spoken of by older community members. Since then, there has been a slow but steady increase in the population. In 1910, an official U.S. government census recorded 78 people. A Bureau of Indian Affairs (BIA) census of the mid-1960's listed approximately 210 Sandias. Investigation shows that of these, approximately 180 should be considered as fairly stable residents, with another 30 to 35 Sandias residing primarily in Utah, Arizona, California, and the Albuquerque and Santa Fe areas. Some of the nonresident Sandias are people who have left the pueblo seeking job opportunities. Others have left because of failure to adjust successfully to the pueblo society and its values. Of those leaving for economic reasons, most intend to return to Sandia in the future.

Undoubtedly, the population increase is attributable in part to improved medical facilities. Basically, however, it reflects the successful accommodation which the Sandias have made to the larger society. The observer is struck less by population increase than by the obvious distinctiveness and solidarity of the community. Superficially, acceptance of American trappings is everywhere. Only a few older men and women wear traditional clothing. Almost every home has a TV set, most families have cars or trucks, all children attend the nearby public or parochial schools, and the traditional farming economy has largely been discarded. Most adults are now participants in the nearby Albuquerque economy, in semiskilled or skilled occupations. An increasing number of young Sandias are entering business colleges, nurses training programs, and universities. Nonetheless, the community is distinctively Indian, retaining much of its cultural heritage and pride. It provides its members with social, economic, and emotional security, so that relatively few leave to attempt absorption or assimilation into the surrounding society. Why is this so?

Part of the answer is to be found in Sandia's strategic location. It is close enough to a commercial American city so that its members can partake in the wider economy, while maintaining residence within their natal community. The 1920's and 1930's were critical years during which there was a steadily increasing shift away from subsistence farming. Sandias became exposed to a variety of material goods offered by the larger society, resulting in a series of desires for goods which could not be satisfied under the traditional economy. Although Sandias did not suffer land deprivation, as did many other Indian tribes, they could not properly utilize their land within a modern farming economy. To compete within the large western market would have demanded sizeable financial expenditures in modern farming equipment. Lacking collateral, Sandias could not obtain loans. An experimental government nursery, however, was set up on Sandia land from the late 1930's through the 1940's, to introduce Indians to modern farming techniques. Although it employed a large percentage of Sandia males, they would not or could not take advantage of the education provided and their own lands were neglected in many cases. Only a few Sandias have continued to farm as a major source of support.

During the 1940's, some Sandias served in the armed forces. This furthered the drift away from farming while it simultaneously increased exposure to outside material goods. The final result for Sandias has been incorporation into the general labor market, with most working for the nearby BIA, in commercial enterprises, or for the Albuquerque service and utilities companies. Occupations include linemen, draftsmen, truck operators, laborers, and jewelry craftsmen. The shift away from farming was facilitated by an accommodation on the part of employers of Indians, many of whom allow the periodic absenteeism which is necessary so that the Sandias may continue to participate in their traditional ceremonial activities. The surplus of land resulting from the shift away from farming is partially siphoned off through leasing, with the proceeds returned to the community.

There has been, then, a drastic change in the economic dimension of Sandia life, although the shock has been cushioned by territorial maintenance. This kind of balancing is one form of accommodation which allows the community to remain essentially intact. Another kind of accommodation has to do with the avoidance of a generation schism between conservative and progressive elements, so that the pueblo has not been split into an older, rigid, orthodox faction in conflict with a younger group rejecting traditional values.

Evidently, there was a period when this kind of split was a potential danger. Middle-aged informants speak of a mistrust of the whites which their parents sought to instill in them. Many were told not to speak to Anglo strangers and not to converse among themselves in English. In the mid-1930's, a nativistic movement developed briefly in the pueblo, during which conservative parents sought to keep their children out of the schools and in the community. By and large, those who succeeded in this brought to maturity the economically less successful Sandias, while those who encouraged their children in the education of the larger society reared a group able to participate successfully in the western economy. Throughout this transition period, the latter group maintained its basic respect for the older members, deferring to them in ceremonial matters or where behavioral disputes arose.

A complex system of intergenerational adjustment and accommodation has resulted. The older generation has developed a respect (albeit sometimes begrudging) for the judgment of the younger generation, particularly where matters involving exter-

nal relations are concerned. Younger Sandias look (albeit sometimes condescendingly) to the older people as repositories of wis-
dom developed with the passage of time. Informants state that, in
council, it is the word of the older people that is decisive. Younger members, however, make their opinions known; these are
weighed by the elders, and then mediated to the pueblo at large
as if from the lips of the older ones. Thus, the prestige of the
older generation is maintained, although its opinions are subtly
tempered.

The process of balancing younger and older elements is evident
in various parts of the social system. It results in a meaningful
allocation of roles to Sandias throughout the age spectrum. Two
parallel authority structures interact at strategic points in the
pueblo. One is the religious hierarchy, concerned with the maintenance and transmission of native religious practices. It is
headed by the cacique, who occupies the most sacred position in
the pueblo. Below him are several apprentices, men who will
eventually succeed him. At the present time, the cacique is one of
the oldest men in the community, while his apprentices represent
the middle-aged and younger age groups. Below the office of
cacique are two other important ceremonial positions, of approximately equal importance. These, too, are filled by older men.
Beneath these is the office of war chief, presently occupied by an
older, respected man, who, together with his assistants, acts as liai-
son between the cacique and the pueblo at large. This post is also
a meeting point with the secular administration, consisting of an
annually-appointed governor, a group of officers who assist the
governor, the lieutenant governor and his assistants, and an offi-
cer of the whip, who is authorized to administer physical punishment to recalcitrant pueblo members.

Today, there is a tendency to select the governor and his lieutenant from among the more educated and articulate Sandias,
since these posts mediate between the pueblo and the outside
world, including local, federal, and other Indian tribal governments. A critical juncture of these two hierarchies is found in

deliberative and judicial bodies, which draw members from both hierarchies to act as a council or court of minor offenses. These bodies include past religious and secular officials. Significantly, these major authority structures provide roles for all the community's adult males and act as training grounds in which young and old constantly interact. That the most revered authority position is religious, and is capable of influencing behavioral matters, is an important factor in shielding Sandia from the more secular and variable values of the larger society; that the cacique has the final word in appointing the governor balances the growing importance of the latter post because of its external dealings.

The Sandia secular government has also enlarged to accommodate its increased interaction with United States government agencies and with other tribal groups. In addition to long-standing ties with the Bureau of Indian Affairs, Sandia participates in the All-Indian Pueblo Council, a group interested in bettering the lot of southwestern Indians generally. Sandia is represented at these meetings by its governor and a few men whom he appoints to accompany him. It is noteworthy in this connection that a teenage group of boys and girls has formed at Sandia, its purpose being to promote awareness of the Indian's role in the modern world. The group is now represented in Sandia's own councils and some of its members attend the larger tribal Indian meetings. Evidently, these Sandia teenagers are responding to outside pressure by intensifying their loyalty to Sandia and Indians generally, while attempting to strengthen and redefine their position.

In addition to these political ties, Sandia participates in a Community Action Program (CAP) sponsored by the Office of Economic Opportunity. The program is attempting to bring educational and social benefits to Indians through their direct participation. In this respect, it departs from the more paternalistic procedure of the Bureau of Indian Affairs.

Sandia response to the program is interesting. Many approve of replacing welfare programs with more communally cooperative

endeavors, which would employ males needing jobs instead of al-
lowing them to subsist on government doles. Although it would
be premature to do more than note this reaction, it does perhaps
suggest that some Sandias are concerned with retaining their dignity through self-reliance. It is noteworthy as well that the Sandia
CAP coordinator, a young man, has commented to this investigator about the desirability of initiating a course for Sandias which
would instruct them in their own history, traditions and their
language. Many young Sandias are no longer fluent in their native tongue. The loss of their language would, of course, pose a
threat to the maintenance of their cultural heritage. Whether such
a program will come to fruition is questionable. However, there is
evidently a growing conscious concern, on the part of some Sandias now reaching maturity, to ensure their cultural survival
and to find programs with which to accomplish this end.

Various other features of Sandia social organization contribute
to its present solidarity. Children are early indoctrinated with
important values and identified with lifelong groups through
ceremonial practices. At birth, they become members in one of a
number of clans. Membership is determined by their mothers'
affiliation. The clans perform functions associated with sickness
and death, providing comfort and a sense of loyalty for their
members. Another dual grouping system divides the pueblo for
dancing in a series of periodic traditional performances. Children
of a family are alternated in membership, first to one group and
then to another. A third system of dual grouping aligns Sandias
for yet another important series of ceremonies and dances in
which recruitment is patrilineal—that is, a child joins the group
of his father. Moreover, all children are initiated, usually by their
mid-teens, through a series of ceremonies which open their eyes
to the traditional religion of the society and make them, in a very
real sense, true Sandias.

These matrilineal, bilateral, and patrilineal membership systems perform an important integrating function in that they
counteract divisive tendencies. They join together, in a compli-

cated network, different sets of people for specific occasions. A
Sandia will mourn with one set, perform fiesta dances with another set, and carry on an important series of dances with yet a
third set. In this way, each Sandia has his own network of interaction with most or all other members of the community. Through
the membership system, a Sandia builds up loyalties and identification with particular groups; through the initiation system, he is
a Sandia.

Sandia's kinship system is also important in tying its members
to the community. A Sandia belongs to a small domestic group,
to a larger kindred which includes grandparents, aunts, uncles,
and cousins, and to the group of all Sandias, most of whom are
related in one way or another. Informants say, "We are all
family."

The domestic group is an important cooperative unit. While
the majority of them consist of parents and children, many are
augmented by grandparents, grandchildren, siblings, nephews,
nieces, and distantly or unrelated people. One is struck by the
fact that all members of such a household are usually involved in
its maintenance. Grandparents are useful in caring for the children of working mothers; mothers are either busily engaged in
rearing their own children or other related youngsters or are
themselves working to contribute to the family budget. Children
past the age of seven are given increasing responsibility in such
chores as housecleaning, wood gathering, house plastering, or
baby-sitting for younger children. Flexibility in the composition
of the domestic unit provides important social security, as no
Sandia, adult or child, need be left destitute or uncared for. Il-
legitimate children, who in our society are usually placed in unrelated homes, are cared for by their own mothers, grandparents,
aunts, or even neighbors, who may want an extra hand in the
family.

The larger kindred group creates a pool from which Sandias
may draw economic or other assistance. This is the group to
which each Sandia belongs by virtue of relationship to a wider

variety of kin than that found within his own household. It is within such a group that a good deal of day-to-day reciprocity is found. Investigation shows it to be the gift-giving group, particularly at Christmas, as well as the group which assembles to discuss behavioral issues of members. It may be an important vehicle for social control.

The third group, that of all Sandias, shows its cooperation at innumerable occasions throughout the year. Events such as weddings find all Sandia households involved in contributing and preparing food for the wedding feast, while most will also provide gifts to give the couple a start. The same intrapueblo interaction is noticeable on other occasions, such as a baptism, during illness, or at death.

There are no historical documents to indicate the earlier kinship system of Sandia. It is possible that there were larger, cooperative household units and a more extensive clan system. Nonetheless, interesting parallels and contrasts may be made between the present system and the American family system. In both, a small nuclear family is the central focus. Extensive family ties in the American system have dwindled in response to the needs of a changing, industrial, mobile society; the male head is ready to change occupation and residence as economic demands require. A large extended family, incorporating several generations, is outmoded. At Sandia, there is also evidence that extended residential groupings have dwindled, as the need for cooperative farm labor has decreased. The need for flexibility in family organization, however, has different effects in the two societies. For Americans, the result has been loss of important personal sources of security, with greater dependence on nonfamilistic institutions and important changes in social structure and traditions. At Sandia, flexibility has helped to sustain important institutions and to maintain its traditions.

In meeting the economic demands of the outside world and some of its attendant ills, Sandias find the answer in primarily small household groups where few members become economic drains. If a household does need an additional member, whether as an elder baby-sitter or a younger chore helper, it may add a member to its household for this purpose from the larger pool of relatives available. Should a family be too large to receive adequate care and support, it may call on a willing grandparent, sibling, or other relative to alleviate the problem. Investigation shows that children are often given a choice of residence. Many informants have pointed out cases where preference is given to a grandparent over a parent. Apparently, Sandia flexibility in kinship and houshold organization insures the maintenance of its population for participation in important ceremonials and traditions, cancelling out, in effect, the pressures of the larger society. The evolution of domestic groups into the form found today at Sandia is probably a good example of the transformation process in the social dimension.

The feeling of Sandias that they are all ultimately family, coupled with a nonmaterialistic set of values, militates against the division of the pueblo into haves and have nots. It is certainly true that some households have more in the way of economic and material comforts. There is also a certain amount of competition between households. Informants point out that when one family introduces a new item into the pueblo, such as a water heater, TV, freezer, etc., other families are quick to follow suit. Yet no basic division of the community into a class society has developed. There appears to be no identification of the materially fortunate with the American middle class and none of the more impoverished with the American working class.

Part of the answer to this lack of approximation to American standards is found in a basically different set of values that Sandias have concerning money and material comfort. These are to be sought after, and money is particularly important if a family is to provide its children with educational opportunities. Nevertheless, money does not determine the basic worth of an individual, and any family can count among its relatives monetarily undistinguished members.

In the last analysis, because of the strong sense of relatedness, it is the duty of the community at large or some of its more fortunate members to provide the less economically sufficient members with what they lack. Wealthier households will give aid, in the form of money, food, and clothing, to poorer families. The community itself, with funds gained primarily through leasing land, distributes money a few times a year to all adult members. Prestige accrues to the Sandias who give, and giving has a levelling-out effect. The lack of a class basis to the society, with criteria based on outside values, is an important deterrent to splitting the community and forcing out either the more or less materially fortunate. Most Sandias remain in the community, to help or be helped by each other.

This investigator frequently attempted to get informants to rank community members by their own set of values. Those with more money are not necessarily placed at the top of the prestige ladder. They may be, if they are known for their generosity. My most recent interrogation of a fairly sophisticated community member, in which I asked whether the richer people weren't in fact more respected, elicited the following response. "Gosh no. After all, we are all really family. It's up to us to take care of each other."

It has been mentioned that neither the economically advantaged nor disadvantaged identify with the appropriate class within the larger society. It is equally apparent that Sandias do not align themselves with minority groups generally, apart from a strong sense of identification with other Indians. This became particularly apparent to the investigator following the assassination of Martin Luther King.

Many informants were questioned concerning this incident. The writer casually expressed her concern for the state of the country, the plight of the Negro, and the hostility of many white elements within it. Reactions were various. Some people were but slightly aware of the incident. Of those who were aware, concern centered mostly on the immediate family of the victim. Some Sandias said outright that since he was a Negro, the matter was of little interest to them. Common to all the reactions was the absence of personal identification with the larger issue involved; there was no attitude that the event was part of a general minority problem that included them. The investigator asked many Sandias whether anything that happened outside of the pueblo really moved them in any way. Most gave the same answer. Their primary concern was the Vietnam war, since several Sandias are in the service. Apparently, unless happenings outside of the pueblo impinge directly on them, they remain psychologically uninvolved.

This last observation is borne out by Sandia's more recent reaction to the assassination of Senator Robert F. Kennedy. The investigator again questioned Sandias concerning this event. A good deal more concern was expressed than for the former tragedy. Kennedy was believed by many Sandias to be a particular friend to the Indian, interested in furthering their welfare. Several Sandias had met Kennedy personally in Washington, during investigations into Indian and poverty problems. In this case, there was a sense of direct loss. In addition, the fact that Senator Kennedy was white undoubtedly had something to do with the sympathy generated. Despite the fact that Indians have been mistreated in many ways by whites, there is generally a more positive feeling for whites than for Negroes. (It is interesting to note that some informants directly stated that it was obviously safer to live at Sandia than outside.)

An examination of Sandia recreational activities shows the extent to which they are largely Indian, and particularly Sandia, oriented. Some Sandias occasionally go to the movies in Albuquerque. A few infrequently take their families to a restaurant or go in a group to a nightclub. Such occasions are rare, however, and when they do occur, Sandias remain a primarily separate group, set apart from the Anglos or Spanish Americans among whom they are mingled.

Visiting patterns are also instructive. Sandias do not casually visit with each other or with outsiders to the extent that people of the larger society do. Usually, a visit is connected with a specific purpose, such as a fiesta or special celebration. Individual Sandias, too, occasionally visit with personal friends in other pueblos or with Spanish Americans or whites, but such interaction is far less frequent than forms of interaction occurring within the pueblo.

One of the most important recreational activities is baseball. At Sandia, there is a male baseball team which has been in existence for at least fifteen years. It recruits males from an age group of about 14 through the early thirties. The males practice in a field at Sandia and belong to a league including the pueblos of Santa Ana, San Felipe, Jemez, Zia and Cochiti. The team plays no games with any of the Albuquerque ball clubs. At the end of the season, an all-star team picked from within this league plays off against another all-Indian league. In a sense, the system mirrors that of the American division into National and American leagues and the all-star team. Games are played every Sunday at the various participating pueblos, with most Sandias, adults and children, attending, unless another pressing affair intervenes. Even older women, with no children involved in the games, go to cheer for the Sandias.

Other important recreational activities include bingo games, played at the Sandia community house. At these games, a few Bernalillo friends or Indians from other pueblos may attend, although the composition of the participants is largely Sandia. Usually, the game is sponsored by a group within the pueblo interested in raising funds. The Sandia Boy Scout troop is a popular fund-raising target. At the games, Sandias of all ages are present, babies sitting on the laps of mothers or other relatives, older children participating.

On occasions such as a high-school graduation, dances will be held within the pueblo, sponsored by the parents of the graduating children. Again, this largely involves Sandias, although relatives and acquaintances from outside may attend.

The Sandia PTA is instructive in indicating the essential inwardness of the community. It is composed of the parents of children attending the Bernalillo schools. Significantly, it is a separate parents' group from the PTA of Bernalillo. There is only one Sandia couple who have consistently belonged to the latter group instead of the Sandia organization. They appear to be the exception rather than the rule.

The children attending the Bernalillo schools have social alignments mirroring those of their parents. They attend the Bernalillo dances and sometimes take as escorts Spanish American classmates. However, a recent event indicates the essential separatism that still prevails. Like teenagers everywhere, the Sandia students decided one afternoon to have an unofficial spree and ditched school. They congregated near the river, drank beer, and stayed out late. Concern over this disciplinary infraction led to a council meeting, at which the children were admonished by their elders. Several children were also severely punished by their parents. It is significant that they acted on this occasion as a group apart from the rest of the Bernalillo student body; no outsiders were involved.

Investigation of the composition of Sandia pueblo sheds a good deal of light on Sandia attitudes toward and relationships with non-Sandia Indians and non-Indians. Approximately 3 per cent of the Sandia population is non-Indian, 87 per cent is Indian, and 10 per cent is of mixed Indian and non-Indian ancestry. Of the non-Indian population, three are Spanish females, one is a white male, and the other two are Spanish males.

Until about thirty years ago, Indian and non-Indian marriages met extreme opposition. Examination of early census material shows such marriages to have been non-existent through the 1920's. Even today, this is not a preferred kind of marriage, as non-Indians can never become fully incorporated into the ceremonial life of the community. Lacking indoctrination in Indian values, non-Indians are a potential source of disruption and conflict. However, non-Indians who do marry in are expected to participate in many cooperative activities, doing their share in cleanup campaigns or in the cooking and food-contributing for various occasions. The extent to which they do cooperate appears to be directly related to their acceptance.

The offspring of such marriages, to become full Sandias, must be reared in the Indian and Sandia manner. This means initiation into the ceremonial life of the community. The six aforementioned marriage cases represent phases of adjustment to Sandia. Four are marriages of fairly long standing, evidently successful. Two involve young people, the outcome still in the balance.

An examination of divorced or separated people at Sandia is instructive in this connection. Of eight such cases, 50 per cent of the failures involve Indian and non-Indian marriages. Comparing Indian and non-Indian marriages which have succeeded to those which have failed, 5 out of 7 Indian-Spanish marriages or 71 per cent have so far worked out, one out of two Indian-white marriages have prevailed, and the one case of a Sandia-Negro marriage where the Sandia woman remained in the pueblo has failed.

The above comparison dovetails remarkably with general Sandia attitudes towards the larger American, non-Indian population. Spanish Americans, particularly of the lower class, share many cultural features with the Indians. They share the Catholic religion, towards which Sandias show a range of fealty; most Sandias are fairly knowledgeable in the Spanish language, and a variety of dietary items are the same. In addition, the godparent system is important to both groups. With whites, there has been a good deal of recent interaction, particularly through the labor and market systems, although some distrust remains. Negroes in most cases are frowned upon. Sandias asked to give their preference between whites and Negroes invariably pick the former.

This investigator has no exact figures to indicate the number of Indian and non-Indian marriages which have succeeded when the Sandia has moved outside the community. There are indications that a larger degree of success is possible. This strongly suggests that marital success within the pueblo depends upon the replacement of outside values with Sandia values. Those who do not succumb to such values either move out or never move into the community, so that the Sandia way of life remains essentially the same.

Marriages between Sandias and Indians of other communities involve 17 per cent of the married people. Undoubtedly, such marriages are related to the small size of the community itself and its inability to supply spouses of the appropriate age and sex in all cases. There are five non-Sandia Indian males married in, or 6 per cent of the male population and 8 non-Sandia Indian females, or 8 per cent of the female population. The somewhat larger percentage of females reflects in part the general attitude that a woman should follow the residence preference of her husband. However, the fact that almost as many males as females marry in reflects the relative desirability of Sandia as a place to locate. Its proximity to job opportunities is a consideration here. Most of the non-Sandia Indian males have already been initiated as Sandias. Most of the females, as well, have been incorporated into the ceremonial organization.

The children of these marriages thoroughly participate in the life of the community, while their inmarrying parents are expected to share in all cooperative activities. The investigator has spoken to most of the inmarrying people in question. Most say that although there is an initial period of readjustment, Sandia comes, in time, to be "home." It is the place where their children are raised and where their most important ties are established. Many of the women have expressed amazement at the amount of cooperative, pueblo-wide activity to be found at Sandia, as compared with their natal homes. This opinion was constantly reiterated by a Taos woman, who explained that at the latter pueblo, the range of intensive interaction was much narrower.

Examination of the eight divorce or separation cases at Sandia shows that 3 of the 4 involving Indian spouses represent non-

Sandias. The fourth involves a female who was born at another pueblo but raised at Sandia. Several interesting questions are raised by examination of these cases. All of the Indians divorced except the last-mentioned are from one pueblo. There is possibly a range of similarity and difference between Sandia culture and other Indian cultures that affects the success or failure of personal relationships. (Fifteen of the nineteen cases of Sandia marriages with other Indians appear to be successful. None of these involves people from the pueblo where there has been a high percentage of marital failure.) In the case of the Sandia-Sandia marital breakup, a tremendous controversy was stirred up in the pueblo, with people taking sides in the dispute. Apparently, there is a good deal of social pressure against such a divorce, with everyone in the society being affected. It is almost as if there are degrees of marital recognition, with marriages between Sandias being of a higher, more irrevocable order.

If marital success or failure is taken as one indicator of an interaction range stretching from within Sandia to various segments outside of it, then various statements can be made. The greatest intensity of interaction is, expectedly, between Sandias. It is here that the greatest pressure is brought to bear on maintaining the marital relationship. Owing to a small population and increased facilities for communication, however, marriages do occur with persons outside of the pueblo.

Marriages with non-Sandia Indians seem to have a fairly high degree of success, with almost as many males as females coming to reside at Sandia. Those who do come are largely incorporated into the ceremonial and social life of the community. Property availability and Sandia's advantageous location close to job facilities are inducements to settling there. Of those Sandias who remain in the community and who are married to non-Indians, those married to Spanish-Americans appear to have the greatest chance of success, attributable to a high degree of sharing of cultural features. Marriage to whites has a greater chance of success than that to Negroes. The last statement supports earlier ones concerning the general lack of identification of Sandias with other minority groups.

The Spanish Americans within the community appear not to identify themselves with the Spanish-American Alianza organized by Reies Tijerina. Particularly since the violence associated with him at Tierra Amarilla, those who know of him appear to have lost respect for him. It is interesting in this connection that Sandias who express an opinion concerning the Spanish land-grant claims approach the question humorously. As far as they are concerned, if the Spanish Americans win their claim, then the arguments supporting their claim would naturally lead to the Indians' own prior one—to what they might win.

The description of Sandia solidarity given so far has been presented as a major deterrent to social disorganization in the face of outside pressure. There is no intent, however, to convey the impression that there is no dissension or factionalism within the community. There are factions, but examination of them shows that they are not the result of conflict between progressive and traditionalistic elements within the community.

For certain purposes, the community may be divided into two major conflicting groups, each composed of a few unrelated families and friends, a third "flexible" group whose members align themselves variously with members of the first two, and a fourth "stay clear" grouping. The groups crystallize over conflict of opinion concerning the personal behavior of community members. Momentum is fed primarily by the Sandia females, who obviously find the field of personal behavior one in which they can find an outlet for their own aggressions or dissatisfactions. Living in such close proximity, there are bound to be tensions and conflicts. The situation parallels that of any small town. Sandia, however, like other Indian communities, vests its real authority, in political and religious matters, in its males. The gossip factionalism probably provides a relatively harmless outlet within which women can express themselves. Informants state that conflicts of the sort which they promulgate are not carried into coun-

cil meetings, where males meet with the idea of maintaining
overall community consensus. They say that, despite bickering
between families, all members will cooperate and lay their petty
grievances aside when community-wide functions are in progress.
This is particularly true when a death shakes the community.
There is a strong value placed on total harmony and the repression of personal antagonisms. Informants speak of admonitions
given by household heads to their families to keep the peace during times when conflicting households must interact publicly.

In a real sense, the community factionalism noted here has an
integrating function. It keeps the interest of Sandias turned inward on their own problems and provides channels for the harmless alleviation of emotions. Since it is perpetuated primarily by
women, who are in a sense second-class citizens, its effects are relatively harmless.

In the most critical and pervasive area of Sandia life, that of
traditional religion, the community has intensified its secretive-
ness in the face of outside pressure. This investigator has never
sought information regarding the ceremonial realm, as that
would effectively bar her from continuing fieldwork. To solicit
such material would pose a threat to the community. Other
pueblos which have revealed facts of this nature are deprecated
by Sandias. One such pueblo, in fact, is barred from certain Sandia rituals as a protective measure. Members of this latter community, if they marry into Sandia, must swear themselves to
secrecy toward others of their natal community before being initiated into Sandia's ceremonial life. This writer has been primarily
associated during her fieldwork with Sandia females, who do not,
in fact, know the innermost fabric of the religious system. Men
are the repositories of the system, and the series of initiations
which they undergo when the religion is revealed to them effectively indoctrinates them against disclosing information to outsiders.

However, certain facts are common knowledge and do not represent a betrayal on the part of the writer. The Sandias, like other

Pueblo Indians conquered by the Spaniards, have a religious life in which Catholic and traditional elements are complexly intertwined. Traditional Indian dances are performed at the church at Christmas, while a fiesta to their patron saint displays the saint prominently in the plaza where traditional native dances are being performed. All Sandias are baptized and take communion, in addition to initiation into the native religion. As with any religious group, there are varying degrees of loyalty and fealty. In general, Sandias can be classified into three main religious types. At one extreme, there are Sandias who are almost exclusively traditional in belief, with only a lightly-worn overlay of Catholicism. In a middle range are Sandias who have strong ties to both Catholicism and the traditional religion. The third class comprises Sandias who are casual about both the traditional and Catholic systems. There appears to be no exclusively Catholic group.

By and large, the Catholic elements do not effectively forge an identification on the part of Sandias with Catholics outside of the community as a minority group. Some Sandias do have godparent relationships with Indians or Spanish Americans in other communities. Most such relationships, however, are established within the community, forging yet another solidary link between Sandias. As for the traditional religion, regardless of the lip service paid to it or the amount of real knowledge that participants have of it, it is a pervasive enough force to create a psychological barrier between the Sandias and the larger society. Three basic elements appear to be involved in maintaining the barrier—pride, humility, and guilt—all of which militate against the acculturation of Sandias into western society.

The pride that Sandias feel towards their religion subtly affects their self-image. It results in a strong ethnocentrism, an extreme form of the "chosen people" complex. In this respect, there are parallels with the Orthodox Jew's image of himself and his people. The view is seldom explicitly stated, but when Sandias are pressed they convey the impression that they are separated

from other human beings by an insuperable gulf. Even if it were
admissible to reveal traditional religious rites and beliefs, they
believe that outsiders could not understand them. The separatism
that Sandias feel stems in part from a feeling of race as a basic
differentiating factor, but added to this are other psychological
components.

Sandias are early trained to submerge their individual identi-
ties for the sake of group loyalties. In practicing their religion,
they are taught to humble themselves in many ways. Since ethics
and religion are inextricably intertwined, behavioral infractions
on the part of a Sandia may lead to dire consequences not only
for himself but for the entire community. The latter might then
find it necessary to be ritually purged of evil. In the process, the
individual offender must frequently be stripped bare, so to speak,
before other members of the community. The investigator has
frequently been told that if an individual will just admit his
wrongs, he will be forgiven. He may have to undergo physical
punishment in the process. The end result is to keep most Sandias
in line. Those who cannot bend their individual personalities to
the system leave. The majority, who remain, are strongly bound
to the community and its religious values. Although the intensity
of conscious belief in the religious system may vary, there is built
up, along with humility, a far-reaching sense of guilt. Sickness
and misfortune are frequently referred to as the result of im-
proper behavior. One informant with whom the writer has
worked closely always attributes her troubles to the fact that she
has been "bad."

Many contrasts are evident here between the Sandia and the
outsider. Whereas Americans generally believe that "truth" is to
be sought through knowledge, Sandias, particularly those who
know the religious system, already have the "truth." Undoubtedly, this is one reason why younger, educated Sandias can still
look to the "uneducated" religious elders. Western education
seems to be valued from a strictly utilitarian viewpoint: it leads

to better jobs. The pursuit of knowledge for its own sake, however, appears to have little meaning for Sandias. They already have their metaphysical system.

In addition, the submergence of the individual within the system is diametrically opposed to our competitive notions. For a Sandia, material striving brings prestige only if the fruits of his strivings are redistributed to his relatives and to the community. As a result, the Sandia enters into our market system not to find a total way of life but merely to sustain his own. Moreover, while members of the larger society practice an ethic of the market largely divorced from any religious ethic, this separation is less extensive for a Sandia. A degree of separation has obviously developed in the wake of growing participation in the larger economy. That such separation has been possible for the Sandia depends perhaps on a successful type of psychological compartmentalization. The Sandia conducts himself one way when he leaves the community to make his living. This is a matter of expediency. But he picks up his real values and personality when he reenters the village in the evening.

The fact that the Sandia has been able so far to compartmentalize in the action sphere, without destroying his basic value system, may not be typical of all Indians. There are many Indians, particularly the more educated, who find the clash of cultures too difficult to adjust to. Frequently, the response is alcoholism. It is noteworthy that at Sandia there appears to be no correlation between degree of education and alcoholism. In fact, a superficial review of cases indicates that it is predominantly within the uneducated element that alcoholics are to be found. However, it does suggest that the degree of overall solidarity of the environment within which minority group members operate is as much a cause of adjustment to outside pressures as it is an effect.

Comparison of the role of guilt between the Sandia and the member of the larger society leads to interesting speculation. All societies instill guilt in their members as part of the indoctrination process into their value systems. In contemporary Western society, however, there is an increasing tendency to view guilt as an immature hangover from childhood training. The emphasis is on freeing the individual from repression so that he may find his own identity. This trend has not made appreciable inroads at Sandia—an individual's identity is still largely to be found within the group. Obviously, the degree of guilt imposed on the Sandia has not been overly malfunctional, in the sense of paralyzing him for purposes of participation within his own culture. It is strong enough, however, to tie him effectively to his community and to bar him from disclosing and dissipating its secrets.

I have mentioned that Sandia may not be typical of all Indian communities. The conditions prevailing at Sandia which allow it to perpetuate its traditions may not be general. It is small in size, so that face-to-face interaction and immediate and constant behavioral control by those in authority are possible. Sandia has been able to keep its land intact. Although much of it is no longer utilized for farming, a good deal of it is leased out by the community, which acts as a kind of corporate group in this respect. The financial returns of this corporation are then redistributed to benefit community members. Perhaps most important in this connection is the fact that Sandias can maintain a strong sense of territoriality. They have always a "national" home, while tax-free property on which to build their domestic homes is readily available.

The fact that Sandias have been able to maintain their territory while participating in the larger economy is undoubtedly another critical condition for their perpetuation. This is facilitated because of the community's proximity to the largest city in New Mexico. Not all Rio Grande pueblos are as strategically situated.

Charles Lange's study of Cochiti indicates that the pueblo, located some 30 miles from Santa Fe and about 40 miles from Albuquerque, is beset by problems that do not occur as frequently at

Sandia.[1] In the former pueblo, a decrease in agriculture has been associated with an increasing exodus to Santa Fe and Albuquerque, where members relocate to enter the labor market. They are no longer under the immediate control of pueblo authorities and their participation in community ceremonies, particularly native ceremonials, has dwindled. Lange states that pueblo residents who visit the homes of the absentees become envious of the noted conveniences. "The power of money is emphasized repeatedly in many situations, causing increased exodus from the village to wage-paying opportunities." [2]

The strong solidarity still apparent at Sandia has been described. Part of it results from the provision of important roles and participation in the political, religious, and kinship structures of the community. The mode of recruitment into these structures and their interlocking nature militates against community schism into permanent factions. The fact that older Sandias maintain important authority in the religious system, in the council, and in the selection of secular officials, albeit recognizing the opinions of younger Sandias, is critical in the avoidance of intergenerational conflict. Some pueblos have adopted an elective system of civil officers, which provides, in effect, the machinery for the polarization of conflicting values. Such machinery, closer to the larger "democratic" society, has been avoided at Sandia. Overall consensus within a community regarded as "family" remains the ideal.

Sandia continues to be an important source of social security for its members. As a corporate group, it engages in land-leasing ventures with returns redistributed in the form of periodic household subsidies, educational assistance, outright gifts to needy members, and community building and repair projects.* It pro-

---

* This does not mean that U.S. government welfare projects have not made inroads. Some Sandias are on welfare, some participate in the government food stamp program. This has led to instances of decreased responsibility

vides tax-free land and free rent, incentives for Sandias to remain in the village and undoubtedly a factor in attracting inmarrying males. Its role as a business corporation appears to be expanding. A fairly new land-leasing venture involves land leasing for the Sandia tramway. Moves are now underway to offer land for industrial sites. One such pending venture includes agreements to hire Sandias as employees. Reticence on the part of older council members to utilize their land in this profitable manner appears to be disappearing as the more educated Sandias are able to convince them that with proper legal safeguards, they will not lose the land or be taken advantage of unfairly by the larger society.

Sandia values operate to prevent identification of elements within the community with similar ones outside. Thus, a lack of class identification based on a monetary standard so far persists. The continuance of cultural differences between the Indians generally and other minority groups effectively combats such alignments. There is undoubtedly a factor of pride which militates against Sandias aligning themselves with racially downtrodden elements, particularly Negroes, and against considering themselves as having the same kinds of problems. Sandias can point to a long history of common tradition, common territory, common social values. The same cannot be said of the heterogeneous group of American Negroes who were drawn from various cultural milieus in Africa and exposed to a variety of environments in this country.

Opposition to recent federal civil rights legislation on the part of Sandias and Indians generally points up this difference. Prompted by recent Negro demands for equal justice under the law, and failing to understand the different philosophy of justice held by the Indian and members of the larger society, a misguided attempt was made to bring the Indian court system more

---

on the part of relatives towards each other. It has not, however, supplanted the role of the community and family as security sources.

into line with the western ideal. Under this system, all minority groups would have the same recourse to our courts. However, while the Negro desires to be a part of this court system, the Indian, including the Sandia, does not. Sandias have evolved, over a long period of time, their own precedents and procedures for dealing with behavioral infractions. Aside from major crimes, they wish to retain their own workable system of justice. It is obvious that in many areas they consider themselves to be distinctive and do not appreciate efforts to blur that distinction.

In addition to a lack of class or minority group identification with elements outside of the pueblo, there is an absence of strong religious identity with the Catholic establishment. In discussing religious groupings at Sandia, it was noted that three major groups could be separated out—strongly traditionalistic, strongly Catholic and traditionalistic, and a group combining weak blends of the two. No exclusively Catholic element prevails, either to split the pueblo or to align itself actively with the outside church. Such a situation has developed at one of the nearby Rio Grande pueblos, causing intracommunity conflict and outside interference.

Sandias, in addition to their Indian commitment, are jealous of their distinctiveness as Sandias. They take pride in noting that Indians from other communities like to attend their dances, as they are considered to be especially well costumed and performed. They take steps to prohibit some Indians from attending certain rituals, thus keeping their secrets from leaking out to the larger society.

It is impossible to predict what will happen to Sandia in the future. Increase in size could conceivably lead to a lessening of controls over individuals and to formation of divisive factions aligning themselves to the outside. Educational exposure could become an important vehicle of change. Whereas it is now viewed largely as an expedient, it could promote philosophical change. However, the forces operating within the pueblo at the present time will surely act as brakes to easy absorption. Examination of the ways in which Sandia is perhaps not typical of other Indian communities is instructive in clarifying some of the variables affecting the range of responses of minority groups generally to the larger surrounding society.

NOTES

1. Lange, Charles H., *Cochiti*, University of Texas Press, 1959, p. 190.
2. *Ibid.*

ROGER W. BANKS

BETWEEN THE TRACKS
AND THE FREEWAY
The Negro in Albuquerque

In the summer of 1905 twenty-nine Negroes met near Niagara
Falls and organized the Niagara Movement. This was the first
cohesive and sustained effort by Negroes to alleviate and eliminate specific racial problems in America. Eventually these radi-
cals, which included William Monroe Trotter, Oswald Garrison
Villard, and W. E. B. DuBois, allied themselves with a small
group of influential white liberals and founded the National
Association for the Advancement of Colored People. Since the
founding of this Northern-oriented organization, the civil rights
movement as a whole has experienced two distinct phases and is
now in the midst of a third. What has happened throughout the
nation and what has not happened in New Mexico can best be
understood through a review of the three phases of the civil rights
struggle.

Twenty years ago the struggle for civil rights and dignity reflected the goals, aspirations and the methods of the National Association for the Advancement of Colored People, America's
wealthiest and most powerful civil rights organization. The
NAACP's persistent efforts, using legal and educational techniques to end racial discrimination met with success in 1954 when

the U.S. Supreme Court handed down a decision overthrowing the separate but equal doctrine in public education. Twenty years ago other civil rights and racially oriented groups such as the Black Panthers, the Black Muslims, the Southern Christian Leadership Conference, and the Student Nonviolent Coordinating Committee were nonexistent. Other established organizations, the National Urban League, the Congress of Racial Equality and the Southern Regional Council were essentially unknown on a national level. Yet today, most of them enjoy national prominence, national membership and considerable publicity. They are not only familiar to most Americans, but because of communication media are familiar to the citizenry of the world.

The major method employed in the drive for civil rights from the turn of the century until 1954 was that of professionalism. The NAACP and other civil rights organizations established during this period (with the exception of CORE, which first involved the individual on a personal level and first initiated the use of the Gandhian concept of direct nonviolent action in America in the early 1940's) conducted civil rights activities via professional civil rights workers.

The significant difference today, compared to the civil rights activities which took place prior to 1954, is that now there is active personal involvement in the struggle for human dignity rather than a reliance on staff professionals to carry out the necessary activities. Today, because of the diverse and changing character of the civil rights protest, the individual Negro can take the initiative, set his own priorities, join the organization which to him seems most appropriate, and take part directly in the activities which he believes will shape and improve his future.

Prior to 1954 discrimination was blatant in the schools, shameful in the area of housing, vicious in employment and belligerent in public accommodations. The activities and programs designed to cure these socioeconomic and political ills were modeled after the NAACP approach and yielded only token results. This first phase of the struggle had lasted for half a century.

The struggle for civil rights and human dignity gained momentum with the successful implementation of the Montgomery, Alabama bus boycott in 1955–56. This event marked the beginning of the democratization of the civil rights struggle. The entire civil rights structure in the South underwent change. The control over activities, initiative, and involvement was transferred from the hands of professional civil rights workers to the hearts and backs of enraged, frustrated militants of every description. Historically, in such periods of democratization, dynamic, charismatic leadership emerges. Montgomery was no exception. The events of the boycott moved Dr. Martin Luther King, Jr., first into a position of local leadership and later into national prominence.

Further momentum developed in the early 1960's when four Negro students in Greensboro, North Carolina, were refused service at a lunch counter reserved for whites. Rather than walk away they quietly and stubbornly refused to leave their seats, an action that came to be known as "sitting-in." This action created immediate responses from students and organizations and unleashed a powerful social force which has disrupted and shaken our nation. It was at this time that most Americans, particularly the Negro, referred to the civil rights struggle as a movement. This sense of movement grew, and with it grew the number of civil rights organizations, the number of involved citizens, and the pressure on Congress to pass necessary legislation—the 1964 Civil Rights Act and Economic Opportunity Act—which would not only protect the rights of Negroes, but increase their opportunities to achieve dignity and acceptance. This was the second phase of the civil rights struggle.

The NAACP's legalistic-educational approach used during the first phase of the civil rights struggle and the direct nonviolent action approach used by SNCC, SCLC and CORE during the second phase were assimilation methods with limited usefulness and effectiveness. These methods achieved some success but only in areas where a large voting Negro populace was present. Desegregation in the areas of public education and accommodations occurred only where the Negroes had voting power which could be used to determine the outcome of an election. Public school desegregation in hardcore segregationist areas like Alabama and Mississippi, where the Negro continues to be disenfranchised, proceeds at a snail's pace, ignoring the mandate given by the U.S. Supreme Court in 1954 to proceed "with all deliberate speed."

The use of nonviolent direct action to dislodge discrimination in public accommodations was spearheaded by students and other mobility conscious groups within the Negro community. The goal to achieve desegregation in public accommodations was a hollow middle-class goal and its accomplishment provided a superficial sense of achievement for the mobility conscious, holding few benefits for the poor, static Negro majority which did not have the means to take advantage of this middle-class-guided adventure. It has become clear that the problems of assimilation facing the Negro populace cannot be solved through private, voluntary nonpolitical action. Particularly in the areas of housing, education and employment, the Negro community must be organized into political power units capable of effecting social and economic change. Thus it is not surprising that, on a national level, the Negro has become more involved and successful in politics, and that the civil rights protest is well into a third and essentially political phase.

Within a period of twenty to thirty years (1938–1968), the Negroes have become an urban people, thereby becoming a viable political force. The mayoralty elections in Gary, Indiana, and Cleveland, Ohio, are examples of this force. The growing number of Negroes who are becoming militant, embracing the concept of "black power," and the established civil rights organizations which are modifying their platforms and plans of action to a militant methodology are even more powerful indications of the desire for political solidarity among Negroes.

The cry of Black Power has evoked considerable controversy. It has alienated a large segment of the white liberal community,

causing an unmistakable withdrawal of sentiment. It has shaken
the Negro middle class who have been incorporated into the
"white society." Essentially it has brought to the surface the fear,
animosity and mistrust that has existed for centuries between the
black and white communities. Black Power has been belittled,
feared and damned, but it has not been understood. The extraor-
dinary thing about this condition is that the concept of Black
Power is extremely simple and is consistent with the traditional
political course of action taken by other ethnic minorities. Both
the Irish and the Italians used politics through ethnic solidarity
to articulate their particular interests.

What does "black power" mean? It means dignity. It does not
mean antiwhite. It means feeling, thinking and acting black—
and liking it. It does not mean separatism. It means cooperation
with those communities who will cooperate. It is a reaction to the
reluctance of White Power to make the kind of changes necessary
to make justice a reality for the Negro. It is unrealistic to think
that the Negro is desirous of going it alone.

Although the economic system of this nation has prospered
within the past two decades, the Negro's economic and social
plight has improved very little. Since 1954 there has been a drastic decline in the number of legal barriers between the Negro and
full equality. Also during this period from 1954 to 1968 there has
been an increase in de facto segregation in America's basic socioeconomic institutions. More than half the Negro families in
America have an annual income of less than $5,000. Moreover,
the unemployment rate of the Negro is twice that of the whites.
In some cities, particularly in the ghetto areas, the rate of unemployment ranges from twenty to fifty per cent. To advance economically the Negro must have a solid political base, because the
civil rights struggle is no longer a moral or ethical phenomenon.
It is, for the most part, an economic and political problem.

The Negro is not the sole vocal minority in America. The Mexican-American, the Puerto Rican, the American Indian and poverty-stricken whites are increasingly vocalizing demands similar

to those of the Negro. Funds to carry out meaningful antipoverty programs, employment training, adult basic and higher education, and adequate housing programs for the benefit of these disadvantaged groups in an egalitarian manner will not be made available, unfortunately, until appropriate pressure is put on Congressional representatives to support such measures or replace representatives with those who will. Having a political base of operation is essential if the Negro is to survive the third phase of the civil rights struggle. And he must also have allies. Above all, he must be understood if there is to be racial harmony in America. These prerequisites have been partially attained in some parts of this country—but not in New Mexico.

The Negro in New Mexico, and particularly in Albuquerque, possesses many Southern Negro characteristics. He is ambivalent in most of his politics, conservative in his religion, and has been timid in the struggle for racial equality and equal opportunity. This is seen in several areas. First, the size of the Negro population is small. There are 17,063 Negroes in the state and 4,652 in the Albuquerque area, according to the 1960 Bureau of the Census Report. The 4,652 Negroes in the Albuquerque area constitute 1.8 per cent of its total population, but make up over 27 per cent of the total Negro population in New Mexico. Second, there is a larger minority group present. New Mexico has a Spanish surname population of 269,122. Third, the Negro is essentially a newcomer to New Mexico and is somewhat transient and parochial in character; he had not participated in politics where he came from, and has not yet been incorporated into the political system of this state even though the Negro has a strong national lobby. Fourth, the Spanish-Americans have inherited a system of politics based on the *patrón,* or political boss. They have a strong state lobby but are weak on the national level. Fifth, the Albuquerque Negro has had to use the existing dominant political system of the Spanish-American as his only means for making demands on the total political system.

The civil rights movement which began in the early 1960's pricked the conscience of this nation but sowed few seeds of change in New Mexico. This is not to say that no change was needed, or that there was no activity directed toward creating this change, or that there were not some token changes. The role the Negro in New Mexico has played in the struggle for civil rights has been minimal, and national and local civil rights victories elsewhere have left the Negro in New Mexico, and particularly in Albuquerque, without an identity, unchanged and uncommitted.

Albuquerque has had an NAACP chapter since the 1940's. Its membership is small, prestigious, mainly middle class, and racially mixed. Its approach has been educational rather than legal, with the church providing much of its membership and leadership. Its main appeal has been moralistic. The Albuquerque chapter is a defensive organization rather than an offensive one and its victories have been battles won for them by the national organization. Many of the victories had no effect on the local scene and its particular problems. The 1954 U.S. Supreme Court decision is a case in point. The Albuquerque Public School system has never had de jure segregation, but this is not because it was integrationist. The fact is that in the late 1930's a representative from the Albuquerque Public School system offered the Negroes of Albuquerque their own school. The Negro families of Albuquerque refused this invitation to segregate themselves. Although the Negro students were allowed to attend neighborhood public schools, they were not treated as equals. They were forced to sit in the back of the classroom and at graduation time they were not lined up in alphabetical order but placed en masse in the center of the procession so that they could not lead their graduating class in or out of the assembly area.

Albuquerque had only one public high school for many years. When a second high school was built in the late 1940's, the school board gerrymandered the districts by including the wealthy University area west of Yale and north of Central Avenue and by excluding the poorer area west of Yale and south of Central Avenue which lessened the possibility of Negroes and Spanish-Americans attending the new high school. Nothing was done by the local NAACP about this condition nor the housing pattern which is still existing and causing de facto segregation.

Discrimination in public accommodations in New Mexico was eventually outlawed with the passage of the 1964 U.S. Civil Rights Act. The involvement of the local NAACP in this problem area was minimal. The state of New Mexico adopted a public accommodations law in the early 1960's but there was no provision for penalty or enforcement in the law. It was as if there were no law, because discrimination in this area blatantly continued. The attempted action taken to solve this situation was through students at the University of New Mexico, the GI Forum, the Archdiocese of Santa Fe and other religious organizations. Their efforts were in vain because a strong bloc of state legislators from the Little Texas area of the state maintained that such an enforcement and penalty provision were not needed.

Several attempts were made to have a state fair-housing law passed by the previously mentioned coalition. Their efforts again were in vain. A Fair Employment Practice Commission statute was passed, but it was not until 1966 that the state legislature approved an allocation which allowed the Commission to function even marginally. The failures in action taken in various areas and the lack of action in other areas by the local NAACP has caused considerable frustration among the Albuquerque Negroes.

Albuquerque has been limited to one civil rights approach, the local NAACP approach, and it has been directed by middle-class Negroes for the Negro middle class. This has deepened the frustration of the lower-class Negroes because their goals and problems are different from those of the middle class. The differences between these two classes of Negroes are sharp, hindering necessary interaction and mutual concern.

The middle-class Negro resides and is employed outside the

Negro slum areas of Albuquerque. His concern is not integration
because he has become culturally, emotionally, economically, and
geographically part of the white community. His primary concern
is inconspicuously keeping what he has and getting more, and not
drawing attention to the fact that he is a Negro. He has broken
with his traditional black background. The vast majority of Albuquerque's Negro middle class are neither natives of Albuquerque nor from New Mexico. They are, primarily, transient professionals who have come to Albuquerque because it is an easy place
to become part of the white community, if one has the educational qualifications, or because they were employed by certain
firms or agencies which directed that they be stationed in Albuquerque. Because of the transient nature and relatively small
numbers of the Negro middle class, they have provided the total
black populace with little or no leadership. They have exhibited
little or no concern about the plight of their lower-class black
brothers and sisters and have become only marginally involved in
activities which would benefit the total black populace. Because
of these conditions, the black population in Albuquerque lacks
concerned, knowledgeable, committed black leadership and is essentially a decapitated leaderless mass.

The lower-class black, on the other hand, has very little and is
preoccupied with his own and his family's private problems, with
unemployment, and other day-to-day frustrations that mirror the
plight of the lower class. He is desirous of getting out of the cycle
of poverty in which he lives, but is pessimistic about his situation.
The basic characteristics of the black residential area in Albuquerque are poverty, apathy, inarticulate resentments and dormant hostilities.

The most densely populated black community in Albuquerque
is census tract thirteen. It is located a mile south of the central
business district between the tracks and the freeway. By using the
data contained in the 1960 U.S. Bureau of the Census Report and
analyzing the socioeconomic problems that the lower-class black
in Albuquerque faces, the existence of these characteristics and

lack of assimilation into the mainstream of Albuquerque life is understandable.

The Negro population of census tract thirteen, which can basically be described as a poverty-transient area, was 1,218 in 1960. Of the 1,014 blacks that resided in this area in 1955, only 383 lived in the same house in 1960, 328 resided elsewhere in the city and 284 lived outside of Albuquerque and New Mexico. The conditions which the transient residents of this area have to live in have inhibited the development of community and group identity and have had substantial consequences for black political activity.

In 1960 there were 300 Negro families in census tract thirteen. More than 10 per cent of these families had an annual income of less than $1,000 and 38 per cent earned less than $3,000 annually. The median income was $3,719, but there were only seventeen families which had incomes of $10,000 or more. The great majority of these families had resided in this census tract for more than fifteen years prior to the 1960 census. They own their homes and are generally conservative politically, but provide little leadership within their community.

Only 23 black residents of census tract thirteen have four or more years of college. The median educational level of attainment in the tract is 9.9 grades. The leadership role of the more educated blacks is minimal. They have participated little in politics and are almost totally absent in community action and development activities.

Of the 326 occupied housing units in census tract thirteen in 1960, 61.6 per cent were categorized as deteriorating or dilapidated. Employment conditions and opportunities facing the blacks in this community are on much the same order. There were 517 employed blacks in this census tract. Of these, 450 were employed in marginal income categories as laborers, private household workers, in service occupations and in clerical-sales positions. The black unemployment rate is estimated at over 8 per cent, twice that of the white unemployment rate.

After viewing the data from census tract thirteen, one can understand the problems facing the Albuquerque blacks. The conditions which exist in this census tract also exist in other areas of Albuquerque where lower-class blacks reside.

The lack of political involvement and social improvement activity, black leadership, and the plight of not having a mechanism to express their frustrations and aspirations have contributed to the invisible and uninvolved character of the Albuquerque Negroes.

The involvement of the masses in the struggle for civil rights as it occurred nationally has not become a reality in Albuquerque. This is not because there are no racial problems in Albuquerque, but because middle-class leadership is not trusted and is no longer acceptable to the poorer and larger segment of the black community, and because the poor have not developed their own leadership.

It was stated earlier that frustration within the Albuquerque Negro community is deepening. But at the same time, the white's concern about the Negro has quickened. Fear and resentment have replaced sympathy. Opportunities for the Negro in Albuquerque have decreased because of what happened in Watts, Atlanta, and Washington, D.C., and not because of any action taken by the Negroes in Albuquerque. This bit of overreaction has added fuel to the already existing frustrations of the Albuquerque Negro.

Lack of equal employment opportunity, decent housing, equal educational opportunity, as well as police brutality, were some of the conditions which caused the riots that left the ghettos across the nation smoldering these past summers. Conditions conducive to riots also exist in New Mexico and are getting worse. They exist and will continue until the Negro and white communities develop a means, through solidarity and coalition, to deal with these problems.

Because of the unique racial composition of Albuquerque—a small Negro population and the presence of a larger Spanish-

American minority—much of the civil rights action taken has been in the form of a coalition. The NAACP and the GI Forum, the main civil rights organ for the Spanish-American, on several occasions banded together with the white liberal community to achieve a common goal. This was, however, before the Black and Brown Power or political phase. Prior to 1965 and the advent of the "War on Poverty" and other "self-help" federal programs, relations between the various ethnic groups were not desperate, but rarely harmonious. Because of the housing pattern, the majority of Negroes reside in the South Broadway area of Albuquerque isolated from the white community. The racial composition of that neighborhood was basically 33 per cent Negro, 66 per cent Spanish-American and the relationship between the two groups was one of tolerance with occasional undercurrents of conflict. But essentially no great conflict developed because of the lack of opportunity for both minority groups. Both were discriminated against and oppressed. Both were faced with the same conditions of poor education, poor housing, high unemployment and underemployment.

Since 1965, however, the relationship between the Negro and the Spanish-American has become a problem in Albuquerque. This situation is the result of the competition and polarization stimulated by the Economic Opportunity Act of 1964 and other similar federally sponsored community self-help programs, reinforced by petty politics on the part of local program directors and the majority communities. Each year after 1964, Congress has committed an appropriation too small to launch a meaningful offensive to accomplish the enormous task of eliminating poverty and providing equal opportunity. This lack of funds has developed increasing competition and animosity that never before existed between the Albuquerque minorities.

The War on Poverty in the Albuquerque area began in March of 1965. One of the essential components of this program was the organization of the poor. The method used to accomplish this task was the development of the Neighborhood Association plan. Attempts were made to organize all poor communities of the county into Neighborhood Associations. It was the function of such organizations to speak for and involve the poor in the development of community improvement programs to meet the needs of particular communities.

The first phase of this organizational plan brought considerable success: nine Neighborhood Associations were organized. There was a visible desire on the part of all communities to cooperate and busy themselves with the problems of poverty. Approximately one year later, however, factions in each of the communities were bidding for control of the Neighborhood Association. In the South Broadway area, where five associations had been developed, the struggle for control became an ethnic struggle between Negroes and Spanish-Americans. It reached a point where one group would not participate if another group was in control. Some residents would regularly attend meetings and participate in programs in another community rather than participate in their own Neighborhood Association where they had little or no voice. In the John Marshall Community, largely census tract thirteen, the confrontation grew to such a point that the Spanish-Americans withdrew and developed their own organization rather than deal with the largely Negro organization (large in the sense that the black majority controlled the organization which had an active membership of from 20 to 30). The split that occurred between the two ethnic groups was stimulated by the desire for employment in the proposed Neighborhood Service Centers and other OEO county programs.

Since 1965 the Economic Opportunity Board, the Community Action Agency for the Albuquerque area, has employed 204 community residents (121 Spanish-Americans, 67 Anglos, and 16 Negroes) in various positions ranging from program directors to janitors. Other federally sponsored programs which operate in the county, such as Operation Service, Employment and Redevelopment, the Home Improvement Program, the Manpower Development Training Program, the Concentrated Employment Program, the Home Education Livelihood Program, and the two Neighborhood Youth Corps Programs, have employed less than four of the many qualified Negroes who have made application. Their cumulative staff positions total over one hundred and fifty.

The economy of New Mexico and particularly Albuquerque is one which depends overwhelmingly on federal appropriations. The U.S. Government, directly and indirectly through subcontracts, provides and supports the livelihood of approximately 90,000 of the county's population. City, county, and state institutions provide the economic means for about another 20,000. The total number of Negroes employed by these institutions is less than 1 per cent. The median number of school years completed for the Negro is 10.9 years. For the Spanish-American the median is 8.7. Viewing these statistics one would think that the Negro's opportunity for employment would be enhanced because of his comparatively higher level of education. This unfortunately is not the case, because, as previously indicated, the economy of Albuquerque has a political base. It is overwhelmingly dependent on federal, state, and local government appropriations. Congressional representatives support certain measures like the War on Poverty which bring additional jobs into a given area. They refer and recommend job candidates for the openings in the supported programs. The majority of these referrals are individuals who have supported the Congressional representative previously either by providing a bloc of votes or an endorsement. The Negro in Albuquerque and elsewhere in New Mexico being unorganized, inexperienced, and essentially uninvolved in politics would be hard pressed to pay the price for this type of ticket of admission. In order to procure employment under this system, involvement in politics has become a prerequisite. Because the Negro is not involved in politics, his chances for procuring employment are relatively slim.

The government policy of issuing funds to impoverished ethnic groups was expedient and necessary in 1965, but has become out-moded. Federal programs with the goal of providing equal oppor-tunity for the poor, regardless of race, now have led to the revital-ization of the separate but equal doctrine, especially in the area of opportunity. It has increased the conflict between the Negro and the Spanish-American communities. And it has decreased the opportunity for the Negro in Albuquerque to achieve equality.

Within the past year a movement has started in the Spanish-American community, particularly among the League of United Latin-American Citizens, a newly formed civil rights organiza-tion, directed towards social change and developing an ethnic economic base. As Spanish-Americans, they already had a politi-cal base, 26 per cent of the total population of the Albuquerque area and 28.3 per cent of the state population. LULAC has become involved to the point of controlling some of the federally spon-sored programs in this area. The hiring practices of these various programs clearly reflect the perspective of those who are in con-trol. There has been wholesale hiring of Spanish-Americans, not because they seem to meet the established hiring criteria, but be-cause they are Spanish-Americans and such a practice is politically desirable. This quiet Brown Power middle-class movement has had the sanction and support of the established political machine. It has led to the strengthening of the already formed coalition between the whites and the Spanish-Americans. It has also been done at the expense of the Negro.

The potential danger to the Negro in the LULAC movement is not its goals, because the development of an economic base pre-ceded by the establishment of a sound political base is exactly what should be considered as the prime objective of the Negro. The main danger, however, lies in the fact that LULAC's suc-cesses or failures will have a great impact on the Negro and on his aspirations and opportunities to develop an economic and politi-cal structure which will assist him in assimilating into the main-

stream of American culture. If LULAC is to succeed it must succeed not only in procuring employment for its membership but
must also take every possible step to insure that the War on Poverty and other federally and locally sponsored programs, where
LULAC members hold key positions, also succeed. Also LULAC's
success should not be accomplished at the expense of the Negro.
The involvement and hiring of Negroes in the various programs,
particularly in the Community Action Programs, should be considered and expanded. It is in these programs that the black will
be able to develop the political and social leadership which his
community so badly needs.

Ethnic equality in Albuquerque seems to depend on political
strength. Opportunity seems to be achieved not because it is right
or moral, but because of organized voting power. The framework
and rules for operating in this highly political system have been
established. The Negro must respond in a political manner. But
the Negro, the minority of minorities in Albuquerque, has traditionally used the existing political machinery to attempt to
achieve his goals and solve his problems.

The Negro in New Mexico is concerned about meaningful employment, adequate housing and equal educational opportunity.
This concern can take one of three directions. It can explode because the majorities are reluctant to make the necessary concessions; it can result in the Negro becoming more involved in the
established political structure; or it can lead toward the development of a separate black political organization.

The Negroes' frustration in New Mexico has not reached a
point which would give rise to a Molotov Cocktail party. But
their frustrations are increasing at an alarming rate. Unless the
necessary solutions to these conditions are developed, black militants might just persuade the local poor Negroes to face reality.
Such a movement would have to depend on outsiders, for the
most part, because the local Negro leadership is middle class and
is not equipped to rally the black masses.

The Negro in New Mexico could and should involve himself in

local and state politics. But whether this involvement would improve the total Negro situation is doubtful. Using the past as an
indication, involvement in the present coalition between the
white and Spanish-American, unless the Negroes are well organized, would undoubtedly reflect the goals of the majorities and
not the goals of the Negro. A Negro participating in such a coalition without an organized constituency would primarily represent himself and not the Negro community.

Responsibility to a Negro constituency is a prerequisite for the
Negro politician if he is committed to representing, working for,
and achieving political goals which will benefit the total Negro
population and not just himself. But the task of representing the
Negro community is difficult if not impossible if the Negro community is not organized.

The change in the civil rights struggle from a moralistic to an
essentially political level has not been felt by the Negro New
Mexican. The energies which have been spent in search of a new
ethnic identity across the nation lie untapped, dormant and isolated, like most of New Mexico's resources. At a time when Negroes in most other areas of this nation are declaring that they are
Negro, Black or Afro-Americans, desirous of creating their own
ethnic image, the Negro in Albuquerque is breaking mirrors.

The problems of assimilation facing the lower-class Negro in
Albuquerque are certainly problems created by the white community. But they are problems that will never be solved until the
Negro and the majority communities take the initiative. Apathy
is the major problem, but what lies at the root of this condition?
What can explain the fact that, in light of the black activity and
accomplishment elsewhere in America over the past fifteen years,
the Negro's position in Albuquerque has remained static?

The answer to both of these questions is identity—self identity
and ethnic identity. The Negro in Albuquerque wants to be
everything but himself. He wants to be white because he doesn't
know what being a Negro really is like. Not only has the "white"
system robbed the Negro of his African heritage through the in-

stitution of slavery, it has also denied him any recognition concerning the great contributions the Negro has given to the making of American society. The Negro has not only been invisible to the white community but to himself as well. The small size of the Negro population has made this rather easy. As a consequence, the Negro in Albuquerque does not know how to be or have pride in the fact that he is a Negro. Until he realizes a positive rather than a transparent ethnic image, his position will remain static and apathy will continue to muffle his aspirations and goals. A positive ethnic awareness is one where the Negro believes that he is a man and assumes the knowledge and responsibility of being a Negro and thinking Negro—and likes it. Whether he assumes a militant, an African-oriented, or Black Nationalist position is of little importance. This awareness will eliminate the apathy, and muted resentments. The Negroes' parochial existence, and dormant hostilities will be replaced by a desire to articulate and participate in actions which will benefit and strengthen their identity and achieve for them human dignity and acceptance.

If progress and equal opportunity are to become a reality, the Albuquerque Negro must realize a positive ethnic identity and channel this awareness and its energies into a unit, thus creating a source of power. Such an organization, a pressure group, could demand solutions to grievances, attract allies and eventually develop a strong coalition which will adequately reflect and incorporate the Negroes' aspirations and problems. The Albuquerque Negro must develop a politically-oriented organization. But the Negro's involvement in politics must include more than merely exercising his franchise. It must include the capability to initiate and influence the political, social, and economic structures that surround him. He can only do this if he has power. In Albuquerque he does not have economic power, so he can only achieve power through organizing. And the Negro can become organized only when he positively accepts the fact that he is a Negro and acts in his own behalf. By doing this the Negro will destroy the invisible image held by himself and the white system and, thus, force a much needed reappraisal of his position in Albuquerque and produce solutions to his problems.

To some, the development of a Negro political organization would seem contrary to the principles of integration and would increase racial strife. But such an endeavor would essentially provide an acceptable means of releasing the accumulated and future frustrations and provide an approach which would insure economic, social and political equality and dignity and acceptance for the Negro in New Mexico.

CONTRIBUTORS

Henry J. Tobias is associate professor of history at the University of New Mexico.

Charles E. Woodhouse is associate professor of sociology at the University of New Mexico.

Marcel Rioux has edited *French-Canadian Society*, with Y. Martin. He is professor of sociology at the Univérsité of Montréal.

Suzanne L. Simons has been engaged in fieldwork at Sandia Pueblo for several years. She is a member of the anthropolgy department of George Washington University.

Frances L. Swadesh has followed the rise of contemporary Spanish-American movements in the Southwest and has a doctorate in anthropology.

Roger Banks, a native of Albuquerque, has been Manpower Director of Bernalillo County for the Office of Economic Opportunity.